Smoking Food at Home
with Smoky Jo

Best wishes Jo Hampson

Smoking Food at Home
with Smoky Jo

Jo Hampson with Georgina Perkins

Quiller

First edition published in 2012 by 2QT Limited (Publishing)
Dalton Lane, Burton In Kendal, Cumbria LA6 1NJ

Reprinted 2013, 2015

This second revised and expanded edition published in 2016 by Quiller,
an imprint of Quiller Publishing Ltd.

British Library Cataloguing-in-Publication Data
A catalogue record for this book is available from the British Library

ISBN 978-1-84689-234-9

All images by Georgina Perkins (except where indicated)
Printed in Malta by Gutenberg Press

Quiller

An imprint of Quiller Publishing Ltd

Wykey House, Wykey, Shrewsbury, SY4 1JA
Tel: 01939 261616 Fax: 01939 261606
E-mail: info@quillerbooks.com
Website: www.quillerpublishing.com

An introduction by Diana Henry

'I am really thrilled that Jo and Georgina have produced a guide to smoking food. I had a fabulous time with them at Smoky Jo's and, despite already knowing quite a bit about the process of smoking food, I learned a whole lot more.

I really appreciated the excellence of their teaching which was so clear, so thorough. It is great to be taught by people who are masters of their craft but still manage to make it accessible, do-able and fun.

I have been experimenting with hot and cold smoked food with confidence ever since!'

Diana Henry, *award-winning food writer and columnist for The Sunday Telegraph*

The Smoky Jo and Smoky Georgina characters are based on an original sketch by Alexandra Perkins.

These were brought to life, along with the other graphics, by Rosie Winfield. My thanks to them both.

May I introduce myself. I am Smoky Jo and this is Smoky Georgina and we are here to help you throughout the book with useful hints and tips.

Smoky Jo

Smoky Georgina

Smoking Food at Home with Smoky Jo

How to use this book

Whilst the principles of smoking food are easy, there are a number of steps to go through and there are lots of variations and options for you to try. Trying to explain all the steps and alternatives in food smoking can be confusing so I thought I would set out my plan in the list of contents to make it easy.

Our introduction to food smoking

Chapter One – The most important message – smoking is easy, it is an art and it is completely personal to your own taste.

Chapter Two – A little bit of history!

Chapter Three – What is smoked food and what is a smoker?

Chapter Four – The different types of smoking, what they look like and how it all works. In this chapter I have gone through the types of smoking and the basic ways in which you can smoke food, both outdoors and in.

Chapter Five – An overview of the smoking processes. Here I have expanded on the previous chapter and explained the different stages to go through in the smoking process. I have also gone through how to smoke in the different ways, using examples of smoking different foods.

Chapter Six – This chapter is dedicated to the salting processes and I have included a number of brining recipes just to get you started.

Chapter Seven – This is all about ingredients, the herbs and spices that go in your brine recipes with some hints and tips about what goes well with what!

Chapter Eight – Now we are getting to the good bits – this is all about the things you can use to make your smoke. Here we talk about the woods you can use and how you use them to create smoke. I have also included the other things you can smoke over.

Chapter Nine – Here I show you a number of different types of smokers, both commercially produced and home-designed, and suggest the best ways to use them.

Chapter Ten – To smoking! This is the reference chapter. It has all the details – suggested brining times, cold smoking times, hot smoking times and cooking times. It then takes you through the step-by-step smoking process for a range of different foods.

Chapter Eleven – Have a look at all the other foods you can smoke – Go smoking crazy!

Chapter Twelve – This final chapter is all about enjoying your smoked food – with a few recipes and serving suggestions to wow people with!

Appendix 1 – A note on food safety

Appendix 2 - List of suppliers

Index

Introduction

My introduction to food smoking

I started smoking food many years ago and have since read just about every book ever written on the subject. My conclusion is that smoking food is an art. There may be scientific processes involved behind the scenes, but smoking food is a very simple concept. Once this is understood, creating masterpieces of food can be easy and great fun. I love smoking our own food at home and continue to get a kick out of experimenting with different foods and flavours. My aim, through Smoky Jo's and this book, is to make the art of smoking easy and provide enough basic information so that you too can start enjoying smoking your own food at home.

So how did this love of smoking food all start? Well, I have to tell you that it was all Smoky Georgina's fault!

Back in 2000 we were both busy working away on the treadmill – advancing our careers in the police and doing well. Georgina was a Detective Inspector and I was a Chief Superintendent. We were on the accelerated promotion scheme and were rapidly progressing up the ranks. All was on course for our high-flying careers.

At least it was until I came back from having been on a four-day assessment centre for promotion. We decided to go out for dinner and there I was telling Georgina all about the process and the silly questions I was asked (and the even sillier answers I gave back) when she interrupted and said, 'You know that smokehouse in Penrith that we visited?'

'Yes,' I replied.

'Well, it's for sale,' she continued.

'Oh,' said I, and carried on with my tale, somewhat perplexed by the interruption. I continued to drone on about the assessment until the end of the evening when I finished my wine, put my glass down and Georgina said, 'You know that smokehouse that's for sale?'

With some irritation I said, 'Yes!'

'Well,' she said, 'do you fancy buying it?'

It took me about four seconds to look up, look her straight in the eye and say,

'Yeah, go on then, let's do it!'

Three months later we had given up our careers, handed back our warrant cards and left the pension... We had dropped our salaries 85% to go north to run a business about which we knew absolutely diddly-squat. I didn't even particularly like smoked food and Georgina's favourite was smoky bacon crisps!

Having left our converted barn in Buckinghamshire with my cat in a basket beside me on the front seat, I was driving towards Cumbria when the headline on the 3pm news informed me that the first case of foot-and-mouth had just been confirmed in Penrith. I never imagined in that moment of panic that buying the Old Smokehouse at Brougham Hall would turn out to be the best thing we ever did!

We worked at the smokehouse for 3½ years and in that time we built the business up, increasing the turnover 350%; we won 16 Great Taste Awards; we were supplying food halls like Fortnum and Mason, Selfridges, Harvey Nichols, and we were smoking privately for the Prince of Wales. We fell in love with smoked food and with the hands-on creativity of smoking food.

In that short time we became victims of our success. Unable to find suitable premises in which to expand further, a number of people approached us to buy the business. Finally we were made an offer that we couldn't turn down and we sold.

Smoky Jo's!
After selling the smokehouse in 2004, we started another business (Stepping Off, – the subject of another book – 'Life Swap'). When we left the Smokehouse we made sure we had a small mountain of smoked duck in our freezer; in spite of this we soon started to miss smoked food – and smoking food! I started to think of ways to smoke food at home.

One day, I was clearing out some confidential papers from a filing cabinet. I knew that most of them should be shredded. Not having a shredder, I realised that the best thing would be to have a fire to destroy the papers. Slightly irked, I looked at the filing cabinet, saw how old and rusty it was and decided I would just take the whole thing outside and set fire to the papers in the cabinet...

I was about to put a match to it when I suddenly thought: 'I wonder what would happen if I lit a fire in the bottom drawer and put a salmon in the top drawer...?!'

Freddie, the first filing cabinet smoker, was the result.

The first salmon and chicken were smoked a month later and offered at a dinner party for six friends. By the end of the meal, there were six people who wanted to learn to smoke their own food at home.

And so Smoky Jo's was born. We have met hundreds of people on our one- and two-day home food smoking courses – and learned a lot from them! In this book we aim to share our smoking knowledge and experience, and have included lots of simple hints and tips to help you get started and to get the best out of your food smoking.

You will discover that smoking food is a very personal thing and you will quickly develop your own way of doing things, your own preferences and your own style of smoking. Perhaps even your own smoked food signature dish!

So please, enjoy yourself; happy smoking!

Chapter One

Important messages...

The first and most important message I need to impart is:

'SMOKING FOOD IS AN ART NOT A SCIENCE.'

The good news is that this means you can't 'do it wrong'. As long as the food is fit to eat, the only thing that matters is whether you like it or not! No-one can tell you to do one thing for one hour and something else for two hours and to smoke it for four hours and then it will be ready ... because smoking food doesn't work like that.

Lots of things can impact on how you smoke your food: how well you have salted it; how long you have brined it; how much smoke there is; what the weather is like; how much food you are smoking... For instance, if it is a dry, warm, windy day, your food will smoke more quickly than on a cold, rainy day. This is because part of the art of smoking food is to take water out and dry the food. If it is a very damp, humid or frosty day with lots of moisture in the atmosphere, food will take much longer to dry out.

Smoked food is all about personal taste. When we ran The Old Smokehouse, we supplied smoked wild salmon to outlets in London and Scotland. In London, the oak-smokiness of our salmon was quite strong; to our Scottish customers it was at the milder end of the spectrum. Historically the fish smokeries in London supplied a largely Jewish market where a mild smoke was preferred; Scottish smokehouses tended to a heavier, often peaty smoke. The joy of smoking at home for your own personal consumption is that you do not have to worry about pleasing too many people!

This book is based on how we smoke food in the UK. It is a little different from how food is smoked in the USA, Australia and South Africa. Most informative food smoking and recipe websites are American – but don't worry – the principles are similar.

Once you have grasped the basics, you can confidently start having fun experimenting with your favourite flavours, herbs and spices and developing your own recipes.

The last important message is that the fires and the smoke are the really easy part! The real art of smoking is in the preparation of the food long before it ever gets anywhere near the smoke.

Chapter Two

How it all began...

I am re-telling this little story courtesy of, and attributed to, Kate Walker who probably has forgotten more about how to smoke food than the rest of us will ever know, has written a number of books on the subject, and who we were lucky enough to meet at the Old Smokehouse when she unexpectedly dropped in.

Once upon a time, when our ancestors lived in caves, the men would foregather and go out hunting. They would go across the plain and kill a buffalo. Now we all know that you cannot eat a buffalo in one sitting, so they would cut up all the spare meat and store it around the caves. Over time they began to realise that the meat nearer the fire seemed to keep longer than the meat that was near the mouth of the cave. They wondered why – and they called everyone together to ponder on this. Eventually one person put up their hand and suggested that perhaps it was something to do with the smoke...

Now the cousins of this happy band of cave-dwellers lived by the sea. Their men folk would also foregather and go a-hunting. (Foregathering was important prior to hunting, apparently.) They too would go across the plain and kill a buffalo. They couldn't eat a whole buffalo either, so they used to cut up what was left and wash it in the sea water and store it. After a while they began to realise that their meat seemed to be edible for longer than their neighbours, who lived upstream from the mouth of the river. They wondered why and a meeting was called to ponder on this. After the minutes of the previous meeting had been agreed, they put their thinking caps on... Eventually one person put up their hand and suggested that it just might be something to do with the saltiness of the water.

The common thread is the reduction of water. Salt ties up water molecules; smoking necessarily involves the movement of air around the food, which obviously starts to dry it.

And so food preserving began ... and to this day we still use both salt and smoke to preserve food.

When we ran the Old Smokehouse we worked closely and well with the

Environmental Health Officer. Although we knew from our own (and some of our customers'!) eating-past-the-use-by-date experiments that the amount of smoke and salt we used did extend the shelf life of our foods, it was not scientific enough for today's regulations. For the commercial shelf life of smoked food, the correct curing and cooking processes, temperature control and packaging are vital.

However, at Smoky Jo's we are more interested in the flavours you can produce using the processes that have evolved from the historic preservation techniques.

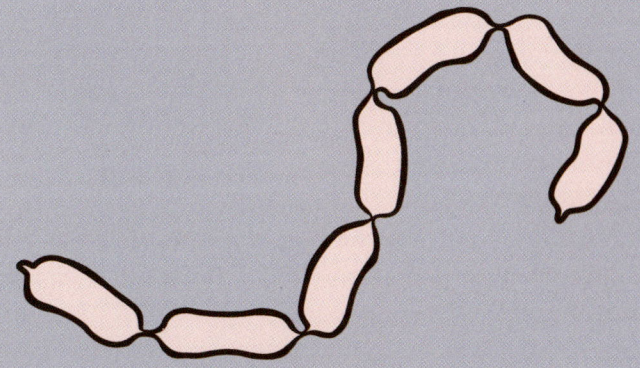

Chapter Three

What is smoked food?

At its simplest, smoked food is food that has been put in a smoky environment where it has been dried and has taken up the flavour of the smoke. To get this to work properly – and to ensure you have the best tasting food – there are a number of things you need to do and in this book we will take you through them step by step.

We aim to make smoking food at home simple. There are lots of things we could tell you about the smoking process: about the interchange of enzymes and micro-organisms; about the chemistry of burning wood; how food is changed by nitrates and nitrites; what happens to the molecular structure of food when it is smoked – and much more – but we are going to keep such things to a minimum. The aim of this book is to get you smoking! So we will explain the two methods of smoking, show you how you can easily smoke at home and give you a number of different ways you can do it.

So let's begin...

What is a smoker?

Or perhaps I should say – what isn't a smoker? Because a smoker can be almost anything from a three-storey building on the side of a harbour to a biscuit tin; from an outside privy to a filing cabinet or cardboard box.

In essence, a smoker is any chamber where you put food and where you can introduce smoke so that the food can be completely surrounded by the smoke – and if you want to hot smoke then you need to be able to heat and cook in it as well.

Got it? Simple!

In the next chapter I will show you diagrams of generic smokers. These will help you understand the process of smoking and how you can smoke in different ways.

Later in the book I will go through a range of smokers, both commercially produced and home-built, to show you how to get the best out of each one.

Chapter Four

How to smoke food

Let's start with the basics

There are two ways to smoke food: cold smoking and hot smoking.

Cold Smoking

Cold smoking is where the food is placed in some type of chamber and smoke is introduced and surrounds the food for a prolonged period of time, without heat. During this time the smoke penetrates the food, the movement of the air dries the food out and a lovely smoky flavour is introduced. Food produced may be ready to eat (such as cold smoked salmon or cheese), or may require cooking (or hot smoking – see below) before being served.

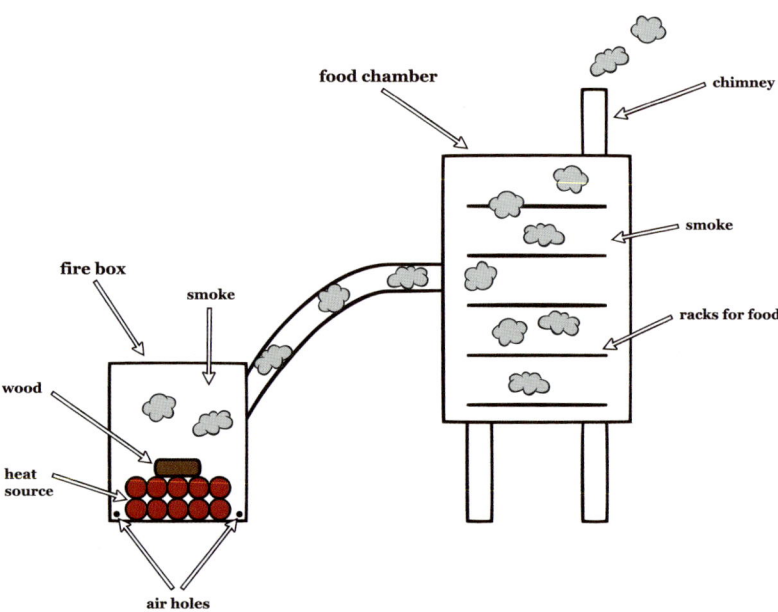

This simple diagram shows how you can easily smoke food. These boxes do not have to be very big – or very expensive. We know some people who use biscuit tins, old tool boxes, old BBQ's, bits of scaffolding pipes and all sorts of other things. It doesn't matter what you use as long as you can create smoke and pipe it through to where your food is.

The important thing here is that your smoke is cool and the easiest way to do this is to have some distance between your heat/smoke source and your food. You need to cold smoke your food in a chamber no warmer than 25°–30°c. If the temperature rises above this, your food will start to cook. Think of smoking a piece of cheese. Anything approaching 30° and your cheese will start to melt!

The heat source suggested in the diagram is charcoal. You put dampened wood on this to create the smoke. You could use just a pile of wood shavings to burn, but these are harder to light and keep alight without perfect draught control. What is important here is that you never have a flame – only smoke.

Lighting fires using only wood can be difficult, so make it easy for yourselves and use a heat source that is cheap, easy to get and easy to light (such as charcoal) and put your wood on top of it. You could also put dry wood on top of a metal plate over a gas ring or electric hotplate – these methods will also create smoke. It is worth remembering that if you put dry wood straight onto heat, it will most likely burst into flame so make sure that your wood is damp (if you're using dust or shavings) or has been soaked (if you're using small logs) overnight.

Hot smoking

Hot smoked food is when the food is smoked and cooked. There are actually two ways you can hot smoke your food.

The first one is where the food is cold smoked first and then hot smoked. The food undergoes a period of cold smoking in the food chamber first and then, while it is still smoking, heat is applied and it is slowly cooked.

This is considered the best way of hot smoking as the food takes on the smoke best at lower temperature – so the smoke has time to penetrate the flesh before the heat gently cooks the food.

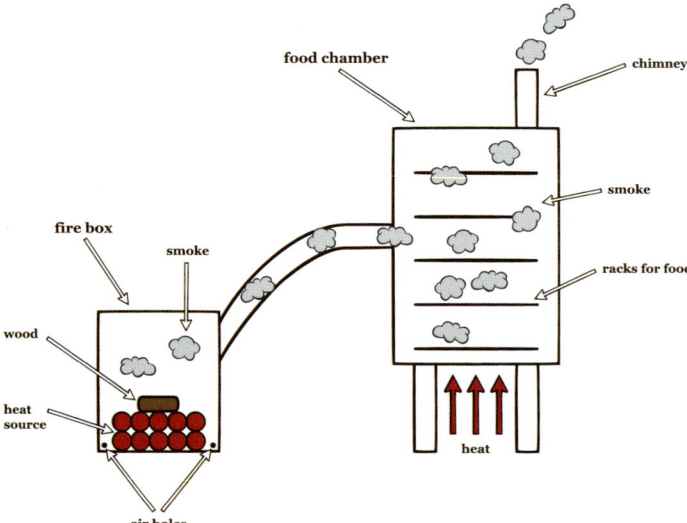

If you do not have the necessary equipment or smoker that enables you to add heat to your smoking chamber, you can always cold smoke the food, remove it and then cook it slowly in a conventional oven, or gently on a barbecue.

The second method of hot smoking can be a much quicker process. Food is placed straight into a chamber where the heat and smoke are. It gets hot very quickly and immediately starts cooking the food, giving it no time to cold smoke. The smoke doesn't have time to fully penetrate the food but is on the outside of the food. To be honest, having come from an artisan smokehouse we were a bit sniffy about this quick method at first, but the end results can be

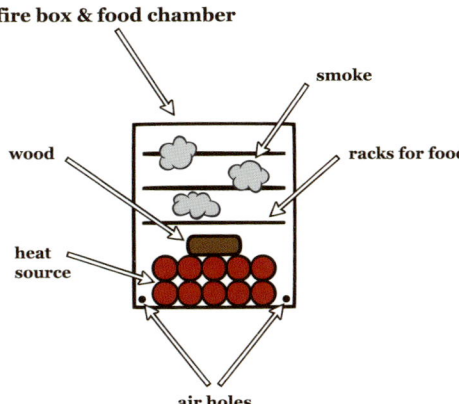

absolutely wonderful and we are now real converts. The food still has a smoky aroma but the flavour may not be as intense throughout. Commercially available smokers that smoke in this way include water-smokers, electric smokers and barrel smokers.

This is another very popular design for small portable or indoor (stovetop) smokers that do the same thing and work on this principle.

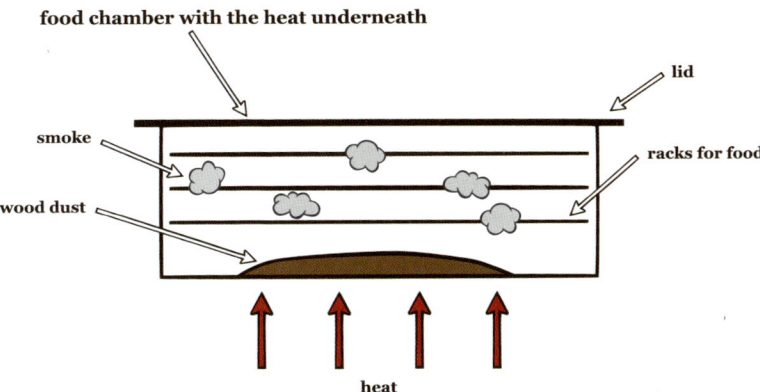

In this design you apply the heat under the chamber and place a thin layer of wood dust on the bottom of the chamber. The base gets hot, the wood gets hot and starts to burn, smoulder and smoke, and the heat cooks the food. These smoking ovens are generally made out of stainless steel, and the principles they use are the same as we use for smoking in the kitchen in a wok or saucepan.

It is really as simple as that. These are the basic ways you can smoke food – and you can copy these principles using a variety of different chambers, heat sources and materials for creating smoke.

Smoking in the kitchen

Some may say you get the best results if you smoke in a purpose-built smoker but you can smoke some wonderful dishes using a wok, a vegetable steamer or a colander in a saucepan!

Smoking using a vegetable steamer

- Simply line the pan in foil (shiny side up) to prevent any damage to the pan.
- Put a small handful of wood dust (or very small wood chip) in the base of the pan.
- Put it on the heat and, as soon as the wood starts to smoke, place the steamer or colander with your food in it into the pan and cover with an airtight lid. (Seal with foil if necessary.)
- The wood will burn away within about 10–15 minutes and then the pan will just be cooking the food. When the food is cooked, take the lid off and serve.

Hot smoked salmon using a vegetable steamer in an old saucepan

Smoking using a wok

- Line the wok with a double layer of foil before adding the wood to protect it and make it easy to clean.
- Put 1 tbsp of wood dust or small chips in the bottom and place a metal rack above.
- Put the food on to the rack, cover with a lid (make a tight seal by wrapping the edges of the wok and lid with foil).
- Put over a medium flame.

- Once you smell the smoke, turn the heat down low and leave the food to cook.

Using this method you can easily smoke mackerel, trout, salmon, chicken or duck fillet, sausages and more... Our favourite for guests is hot smoked salmon that they can flavour themselves before watching and enjoying the theatre of food smoking in the kitchen!

Smoking by making a foil parcel

- Take one large sheet of foil, put your food in and season well.
- Fold the foil over the food and turn it into parcel so the food is completely sealed.
- Take another sheet of foil, sprinkle wood dust or very small chips in the middle and put the parcel containing the food on top of the chippings.
- Take a sharp knife and prick the top of the inner bag 20 times. Fold the outer foil loosely over the top of the parcel and seal it in.

❧ Put the whole foil parcel on a hot griddle pan – or in a pre-heated baking dish in a hot oven – until cooked and piping hot.

This is especially good for cooking thin slices or strips of fish or meat such as salmon, white fish, beef, chicken or eel.

Chapter Five

An overview of the smoking processes

We have already covered the fact that the object of smoking has historically been to preserve food. Since we nearly all have fridges these days, this is no longer the primary reason to smoke food. Now we smoke for fun and for flavour. But, as with all food preparation, we need to know that the food we are preparing is safe to eat.

The first part of food preparation is, of course, selection and acquisition! Smoking will NOT improve or disguise substandard food. Start off with good quality food and you will have good quality smoked food.

We used to smoke fishermen's (and one fisherwoman's) catches for them at the Old Smokehouse. Usually a beautiful salmon was brought in straight from the Eden, silver and glistening, with riverside vegetation still attached. But all too often a fisherman would stand sheepishly at the door and mutter that the fish should have been put back 'but it died', or it was 'foul hooked so I had to take it', or some such tale, and they would unwrap a sorry-looking scarlet cock fish, with no meat left on him that was clearly on its last fins! Optimistically, people thought it would become perfect eating salmon in the magic chamber of a smoker! I had to disappoint them and suggest they fed it to a cat. And I hope they read the sub-text... 'Even if it is the only catch you had all year, YOU SHOULD HAVE PUT IT BACK!'

Part of the food smoking process is drying the food out, firstly with salt and then with the flow of the smoke. This process starts killing off bacteria, rendering the food safe to eat. It also concentrates all the flavours.

As I have previously stated, smoking is an art not a science. I will go further by saying that 'the real artistry of smoking is in the preparation of the food'. By this, I mean the brining or salting of the food. Salting or brining the food before you smoke it begins to reduce the water content. I have only read one book that fully explains the importance of salting – how and why you do it – so I am going explain this in detail, as I believe it is the most important part of the whole smoking process.

There are three reasons why we salt food before smoking it and the first reason is to allow the salt to start the drying process.

So how does this work?

I do not want to over-simplify the process but food is full of bacteria and moisture. The bacteria need moisture to survive and multiply. By applying salt you draw water molecules out of the cells, and as part of this process of osmosis the salt goes into the food as the water comes out.

What does that mean?

Well – in a nutshell – life needs water. If you remove the liquid from food, bacteria cannot multiply and therefore the food will not go off. If you have ever eaten biltong or jerky this demonstrates how total dryness leads to an almost indefinite shelf life. The meat is simply salted and spiced and then hung up to dry in the sun. It dries and dries until there is virtually no moisture left in it. At this point it is completely safe to eat; it has never been cooked but, as there is very little moisture in the meat, the bacteria cannot multiply. So as long as it remains this dry, the food will remain safe to eat. The flavour is also very concentrated.

We, of course, do not want our smoked food to be that dry and chewy. What we are aiming for is to produce smoked food that, in spite of being 'dried' in various ways, is moist, succulent and very tasty.

So, having selected your quality piece of food, you need to start the drying process by salting it. There are two ways you can do this: you can either dry salt or brine it (brine is a salt solution).

Salt dries out food

Dry salt – this simply means covering the food with a layer of dry salt.

Brine – this means that you put the food into a salt solution – a mixture of salt and water. Now this may seem strange as we have been talking about drying out the food, but salt still behaves in the same way even in water. It enters the cells of the food and by osmosis the liquid without salt in the cells comes out. This is because salt goes to the area of least concentration.

When we were running the smokehouse, we could not fathom any reason why you use one method rather than another. It appears to be just personal (or smokehouse) preference.

Chicken fillet in brine

There are a few exceptions to the salting rule.

1.   You do not need to salt food that has already been processed by the addition of salt such as cheese, sausages, black pudding, haggis, etc.
2.   We generally do not salt vegetables before we smoke them unless it is something like an aubergine or marrow which has a very high liquid content.
3.   I tend not to salt shellfish. If I have a weak brine on the go I might pop the shellfish in it, but only ever for about 5 minutes. I do, however, occasionally marinate something like prawns, langoustines or scallops in a little white wine, lemon juice and garlic before smoking.

So let's look at how we use salt in conjunction with the different ways we smoke. I am going to go through the three ways of smoking food already referred to: cold smoking; cold smoking followed by hot smoking, and just hot smoking, by using an example of smoking a different food by each method.

Cold smoking example – a side of salmon

The first step is to weigh the fillet. We need to know its start weight because the best way to confirm that it has smoked properly and is ready to eat is to see how much water it has lost by the end of the smoking process. A loss of 20% ensures that it has smoked correctly. Weight loss is important especially if you are producing food commercially as it gives the food a longer 'shelf life' however it is sometimes difficult to achieve in home smoking so please don't get hung up on the weight loss – you will soon know if your fish is properly smoked or not – just by taste and texture.

My preference for salting salmon is to use dry salt. I lay the fish skin side down on a layer of salt then cover the flesh with salt, being very careful to put much less salt on the thinner parts of the fish – the tail and the belly – than on the thicker parts. The length of time it is left depends on the size of the fish. (For brining times see page 86.) When ready, the flesh of the fish will have tightened up, the salt will be wet and there will be a fair amount of liquid around the fish. This visual evidence shows that osmosis has taken place; the salt has been absorbed into the cells and the liquid has come out.

The next step is to rinse the fish. Wash the salt off under fast-running cold water. You need to get all the salt off.

Finally, blot dry the fish or leave it unwrapped to dry in a fridge or cool place overnight. We want the food to dry out during smoking, but if the food is wet to start with the smoker has to work twice as hard to dry it and the smoking process will take much longer.

Do not put wet food into a cold smoker

Place the fish in your cold smoker and light your fire to create the smoke, and then leave it. Depending on your smoker, the amount of air flow, the density of the smoke, the size of the salmon, the weather and your taste – I told you it was an art not a science! – your salmon should be ready in anywhere between 8–24 hours. The best way to know when it is ready is to weigh it. When it has lost the 20% of its weight it will be done. (It may need longer drying than smoking – see page 95.)

There is another easy test with a salmon to show when it is ready and that is to pick it up. If it is like cardboard – completely stiff so that you can almost balance it on the end of your finger – then it is done.

This diagram shows what I have described with the salmon.

Hot smoking (with cold smoking) example – chicken fillet

You do not need to weigh the chicken. It is not necessary to worry about weight loss with hot smoked food because you will not be relying on the salt and smoke to dry the food to stop bacteria – the heat will kill them.

I salt poultry in a brine solution.

Here is our second reason for salting our food. Smoke appears to love salt. So if you have salted your food and there is salt in the flesh, the smoke will be attracted to it and will penetrate the food. If you do not salt your food, the smoke will not be drawn into it as much, and the smoke will just be on the outside of the food. Whilst this will still give it a smoky flavour, it will not have the richness and depth of the flavour of smoke.

I leave the chicken fillet in the brine for about three hours (for brining times see page 85). Then I rinse it off in fast-running cold water, dry it off or leave it in the fridge overnight. Before I put it in the smoker, I oil the skin, maybe put a bit of flavouring directly onto the skin and then put it in the cold smoker.

Why do we put it in the cold smoker when we are going to cook it? We do this because food takes on smoke best at a low temperature, so putting the food in to cold smoke for a couple of hours gives the smoke time to penetrate the food and gives the food a little while to dry out.

This is also when something magical happens. In my experience, smoking food is not just about adding a smoky flavour to food. When food is smoked properly, the smoke can add and enhance flavours that are not so obvious in the food until it is smoked. The smoke seems to draw out and develop other flavours.

For example, if you smoke prawns you will be surprised at how sweet they taste. If you smoke a Stilton cheese you might find that it tastes a little saltier smoked than it does unsmoked. Mushrooms, again, taste sweeter. I smoked English brie the other day and the smoke brought out a really yeasty taste.

OK, so back to the smoker. Having let the chicken fillet cold smoke for a couple of hours, you can then hot smoke it until it is cooked. For the very best results, you want to cook it slowly at a low temperature while the smoker is still smoking.

Smoke brings out other flavours in the food as well as adding a smoky flavour — and that's magic

There are two reasons for the slow cooking: firstly to allow the flavours to develop more; and secondly, having dried out the chicken with salt then dried it out with smoke, you don't want to dry it out too much more with too much heat! The danger is that the chicken will be like a bit of old leather – and the real art of smoking is to produce food that has been dried out in this way yet is still beautifully moist, succulent and very, very tasty. Smoking over a low temperature is always better than smoking over a high heat.

This diagram shows what I have described with the chicken.

Hot smoking example – whole trout

Again, I normally salt my trout in a brine solution for hot smoking. And here is our third reason for salting the food: not only does it get the water out and take the salt in, we can use the brine to take other flavours to the heart of our food. By adding flavours – herbs and spices – to the brine we can create even more delicious smoked food. I find it far more effective to flavour my food through the brines rather than just by using different woods.

Using a basic brine solution, I will brine the trout for about 30–45 minutes, depending on the size of the fish. (For brining times see page 85.) I then rinse off the trout in fast-running cold water. It does not matter so much about either the weight loss of the fish or whether it is dry or not, as it is going straight into a hot smoker. It is preferable, however, to leave it for at least a few hours before putting it in the smoker to enable the flavours to develop through the fish.

The fish then goes straight into the hot smoker. In this hot smoker the food will have very little time to take on the smoke at a low temperature, so the smoke will barely penetrate the flesh but will certainly flavour the food.

This diagram shows what I have described with the trout.

Food smoked like this is delicious straight from the smoker – but much smokier the next day!

This is a great way to smoke food; it may not have the full depth of smoke flavours but it is easy, quick, convenient and produces a delicious product.

For larger items that hot smoke at a lower temperature for many hours, in a water smoker for example, the smoke does start to penetrate.

Chapter Six

Brine recipes

Whilst it is important to salt food prior to smoking in some way, saltiness of food is very much a matter of personal taste. Generally speaking, the stronger the salt solution the quicker the food will absorb it; some people prefer to use a weaker solution and let the food brine for longer. This is again a matter of personal choice. As you become more experienced in smoking your own food, you will work out your own recipes, brine strength, brining time and smoking time to suit your own palate. Salt levels become more important when food is to be eaten cold smoked only, but even then the drying required to ensure food safety can be achieved in other ways.

It does not matter greatly for home smoking what sort of salt you use. We generally suggest ordinary table or cooking salt will be perfectly adequate. Some people do not recommend using this because it contains an anticaking agent but we have not found this to be a problem. American books recommend using Kosher salt which does not contain iodine but it also often contains anticaking agents. Additive free salts are now readily available.

To help you make your own decisions on your brine solution here are some approximate brine strengths. These will affect the moisture loss in the food changing the texture as well as flavour.

> 57 gms salt to each litre of water = mild solution
> 120 gms salt to each litre of water = medium solution
> 190 gms salt to each litre of water = strong solution
> 270 gms salt to each litre of water = very strong solution

Sugar does a similar job to salt in terms of water removal, though less effectively, and is useful to add to your brine. I use sugar in brines because salt tends to harden the flesh of food while sugar tenderises it. I generally use white sugar in a brine solution but I use demerara or cane sugar for a dry salt cure.

It is important to make sure that the sugar and salt are completely dissolved in the water, otherwise osmosis will not take place and your food will start to deteriorate in the water. This was a lesson we learned when we took over The Old Smokehouse. Our predecessor told us – with visible angst! – of the time she came to rinse off twenty venison joints that had been brining over a weekend;

she got to the bottom of the brine tub and there was the undisturbed pile of salt and sugar, completely unstirred. The venison, having been sitting in water at room temperature for three days, went to waste. A generously shared tale which ensured it was one mistake we never made! Obviously we made a few others...

So those are the basic ingredients for your brine: water, salt and sugar.

There is one more ingredient I should mention: saltpetre. Saltpetre (potassium nitrate) has a bitter taste but is used in curing and preserving as it helps to retain the colour of the flesh and, more importantly, it has a role in inhibiting the growth of bacteria. You only need a very small amount and it is becoming increasingly hard to source. Whilst we used it when we were smoking commercially, we no longer do. In home smoking, where we are generally not smoking with the intention of preserving the food for a long time, it is not an essential ingredient. If you do source some, then by all means use it in your brines – a small pinch to 2 litres of brine.

Now to this base brine of water, salt, sugar (and maybe saltpetre) you can add anything you like. This is where the fun starts!

The following recipes are just to give you an idea of what you can use, but this is where you can start creating your own ideas and recipes that will give you your own unique flavours. We have had some wonderful creations on Smoky Jo's courses...

Sweet Pickle Brine – basic brine for meat, game and poultry

This is a favourite within the smoking trade as it gives a depth to the natural flavours of the food without covering them. This brine simply has pickling spices added to the base brine and I use it for all meat, game and poultry. Cover a tablespoon of pickling spices with boiling water and allow to cool before adding to your base brine.

I am a creature of habit and I also tend to add garlic powder to most of my brines. So my base brine often starts like this:

> 2 litres water
> 240 gms salt
> 40 gms sugar
> (Small pinch of saltpetre)
> ¹/₂ tsp garlic powder
> 1 tbsp pickling spices (soaked in boiling water and cooled)

Into this I will add other ingredients that I like with particular meats, poultry or game. If I am adding liquid, I will reduce the amount of water. For example, I love tarragon and wine with chicken so my favourite brine for chicken looks like this:

Brine for hot smoked chicken
> 1.8 litres water
> 240 gms salt
> 40 gms sugar
> (Small pinch of saltpetre)
> ¹/₂ tsp garlic powder
> 2 tbsp pickling spices (soaked in boiling water and cooled)
> 200 ml of white wine
> 2 tsp of chopped fresh (or dried soaked in boiling water) tarragon leaves.

This amount will do about four fillets or one whole chicken, depending on your container.

Brine recipes

I have included these recipes just to give you an idea of the variety of herbs and spices you can add to your brine. Dried herbs and spices should be covered with boiling water before being added. These are all medium brines unless stated.

In addition to the herbs and spices, I also add flavours through liquids. Using red or white wine, cider, grape juice, or fruit juices such as orange, apple, cranberry, etc. can really add flavour, as can honey, molasses or maple syrup.

All recipes can be multiplied for when you are filling your smoker for a feast or to stock your freezer!

Suggestions for brines

Brine for hot smoked trout
2 litres water
240 gms salt
40 gms sugar
(Small pinch of saltpetre)
$1/2$ tsp garlic powder
2 tbsp lemon juice
1 tsp onion powder

Brine for salmon
3.8 litres water
500 gms salt
2 tsp soft brown sugar
(Small pinch of saltpetre)
2 bay leaves
200 ml white wine
Juice of half a lemon

Brine for kippers
2 litres water
240 gms salt
40 gms sugar
(Small pinch of saltpetre)
$1/2$ tsp garlic powder
1 tsp crushed mustard seed
2 tbsp lemon juice
1 tsp onion powder

Brine for hot or cold smoked beef
1.8 litres water
240 gms salt
40 gms sugar
(Small pinch of saltpetre)
$1/2$ tsp garlic powder
200 ml red wine
6 crushed juniper berries

Brine for lamb
1.8 litres water
240 gms salt
40 gms sugar
(Small pinch of saltpetre)
$1/2$ tsp garlic powder
200 ml red wine
$1/2$ tsp marjoram
1 tsp rosemary

Brine for pork
1.8 litres water
240 gms salt
40 gms sugar
(Small pinch of saltpetre)
$1/2$ tsp garlic powder
2 tsp honey (dissolved)
200 ml apple juice
2 cloves
$1/2$ tsp caraway seeds
1 tsp oregano

Brine for duck and goose
1.9 litres water
240 gms salt
40 gms sugar
(Small pinch of saltpetre)
$1/2$ tsp garlic powder
100 ml red wine
Juice from half orange
2 crushed cardamoms

Brine for game – rabbit, hare etc
2 litres water
240 gms salt
40 gms sugar
(Small pinch of saltpetre)
$^1/_2$ tsp garlic powder
1 tsp mixed spice
2 crushed bay leaves
1 tsp thyme
$^1/_2$ tsp crushed fennel seeds

Brine for quail
2 litres water
240 gms salt
40 gms sugar
(Small pinch of saltpetre)
$^1/_2$ tsp garlic powder
1 tsp chopped basil
$^1/_2$ tsp parsley

Brine for pheasant or pigeon, etc
1.8 litres water
240 gms salt
40 gms sugar
(Small pinch of saltpetre)
$^1/_2$ tsp garlic powder
$^1/_2$ tsp chilli powder
$^1/_2$ tsp mace
100 ml port
100 ml cranberry juice

Brine for venison
1.8 litres water
240 gms salt
40 gms sugar
(Small pinch of saltpetre)
$^1/_2$ tsp garlic powder
2 tsp maple syrup
200 ml red wine
1 bay leaf
1 tsp sage
2 crushed juniper berries

You can also make your own specific flavours to add to salt or brines such as these, which have all been used on Smoky Jo courses!

Tandoori
Coriander seed
Cumin
Onion powder
Chilli powder
Cinnamon
Pepper
Cloves
Garlic
Oregano
Crushed chilli
Ginger

Thai
Fresh chopped coriander
Chilli powder
Ginger
Lime juice

Cajun
Paprika
Basil
Garlic
Onion powder
Black pepper
Cumin
Mustard powder

You can now more readily buy pre-mixed spice flavours which may make it easier.

So have fun, be inventive, try different flavours and see which you really enjoy.

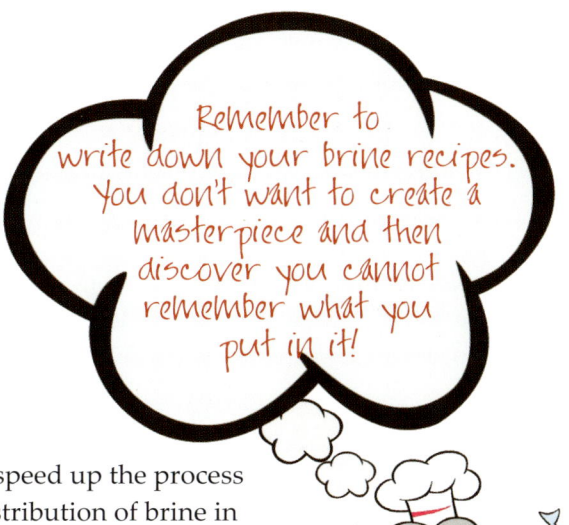

Remember to write down your brine recipes. You don't want to create a masterpiece and then discover you cannot remember what you put in it!

Some people use a brining pump or needle to insert the brine deep into the flesh. This can speed up the process but it can also create an uneven distribution of brine in the flesh which will inhibit an even smoking, or stop an effective smoking taking place. I have never used a brine pump, always preferring a natural saturation process of the brine into the flesh.

Suggestions for dry salt cures

You can use plain salt or be creative with your dry salting by adding flavours.

Dry salt cure for salmon

> 500 gms salt
> 100 gms soft brown sugar
> (A pinch of saltpetre)
> 2 tbsp vodka/whisky/white or dark rum

Some people 'paint' the fish with whisky, vodka or rum before they sprinkle the salt.

Sprinkle dry salt on a board or tray. Place the salmon skin-side down on the salt. (If it is a particularly big fish, you can carefully cut through the skin once or twice at the deepest part of the flesh before putting it on the salt.) Then sprinkle salt over the fish, being careful to have much less salt where the flesh is thinner at the tail and the belly.

I sprinkle a little demerara sugar over the fish as well.

Dry salt cure for cold smoked tuna, marlin and swordfish

For salting tuna you need to cover it with salt and sugar. We use a ratio of 2:1.

    500 gms salt
    250 gms sugar

For cold smoking you ideally need large fillets or pieces of fish. We used to smoke pieces of about 2 kgs in weight. Simply roll the fish in the mixture of salt and sugar, re-covering as necessary.

Dry salt cure or rub for beef

    500 gms salt
    (A pinch of saltpetre)
    50 gms demerara sugar
    2 tsp ground peppercorns
    1 tsp garlic powder
    1 tsp paprika
    2 crushed bay leaves
    1 clove
    1 tsp allspice
    $1/2$ tsp nutmeg

Mix all the ingredients together and rub over the whole surface area of the meat. Turn the meat every few hours, again rubbing in the mixture.

If you fancy making your own jerky or biltong (seasoned meat that has been completely dried) try adding a tablespoon of pickling spices soaked in vinegar to this mixture and leave to mature before slicing it thinly and hanging it up to air dry.

Do not salt food that has been processed, i.e. sausages, cheese, black pudding, etc or vegetables, nuts and olives ... but do smoke them!

Don't brine food that has already been processed

Write your brine recipes here!

Chapter Seven

Herbs & Spices

As with all cooking, there is joy in experimenting with flavours. You can discover and create new smells and tastes by using a wide variety of herbs and spices in your brine recipes.

In addition to using flavours in rubs, brines and marinades you can also use them with your smoking material. Mix herbs or spices into wood shavings or dust, tea or rice, or simply sprinkle them on your wood or charcoal to add interesting aromas.

We have found that the best way to get the flavours of herbs into your brine is to soak them in a little boiling water and then add the mixture to your brine. This process releases the flavours of the herbs and will increase the flavours to your food.

The flavours of some herbs and spices complement particular foods. Below is a general list giving the spice or herb, its flavour, the best form to use, and an idea of some of the foods we recommend you use them with.

Herbs

Herb	Flavour	Form	Recommended Use
Basil	Strong, pungent and sweet	Fresh or dried	Lamb, all poultry and fish. Good with tomato
Bay Leaf	Aromatic, can be bitter	Whole, crushed or dried	In all brines and marinades
Chervil	Aromatic. Fragrant and delicate	Fresh or dried	All shellfish, fish, poultry and white meat
Dill	Sharp and fragrant, slightly sweet	Fresh or dried	Salmon and seafood
Fennel	Aniseed flavour. Fragrant	Whole or crushed	Fish, lamb, poultry and vegetables
Garlic	Strong smelling. Pungent taste	Granulated, ground or crushed	In all brines and marinades
Lemongrass	Lemony, strong and flavoursome	Fresh, dried or paste	Fish, poultry, white meats
Marjoram	Musty, spicy and sweet	Fresh or dried	Fish, game, meat, especially lamb

Herb	Flavour	Form	Recommended Use
Mint	Refreshing flavour, spearmint	Fresh, crushed or dried	Fish, lamb and mutton
Oregano	Strong, spicy and sweet	Fresh or dried	Fish, poultry and white meat
Parsley	Fragrant and refreshing	Fresh or dried	All brines and marinades
Rosemary	Fragrant and pungent. Slightly resinous	Fresh, crushed or dried	Strong fish, lamb
Sage	Pungent, strong, aromatic	Fresh or dried	Poultry and venison
Tarragon	Strong, aromatic bitter-sweet	Fresh or dried	Fish, poultry and game
Thyme	Strong and pungent	Fresh or dried	Fish, meat poultry and game

Spices

Spice	Flavour	Form	Recommended Use
Allspice Whole or ground.	Aromatic with a mixture of flavours - cloves, nutmeg and cinnamon	When using whole berries crush before use	Add to rubs or use in brines and marinades. Beef, pork and lamb
Aniseed	Mild liquorice smell and flavour	Ground	Seafood and mild game. Sausages
Caraway	Sharp, peppery and slightly bitter	Use whole or ground	Rich meat and game. Goose and pork. Sausages
Cardamom	Lemony and bitter-sweet	Open and grind	Strong meat, game, goose and sausages
Cayenne Pepper	Hot and tangy	Ground	In all brines and marinades
Celery salt	Bitter celery-like flavour	Granules	Sparingly in brines. Sausages

Spice	Flavour	Form	Recommended Use
Chillies	Strong and peppery	Use whole, ground or crushed	All recipes requiring a strong hot taste
Cinnamon	Sweet, musky, spicy flavour	Whole sticks, ground or crushed	Salmon with maple, sprinkled on meat, or with curry flavours
Cloves	Pungent, sweet and tangy	Use whole	In brines for meat, game, duck, goose and ham
Coriander	Mild and sweet	Chop fresh leaves. Ground has a lemony flavour	In brines and rubs for poultry and meat
Cumin	Strong and aromatic with a lasting flavour	Ground	In brines and rubs for lamb and beef. Sausages
Fenugreek	Slightly bitter	Use whole	Oily fish
Ginger	Rich, hot and pungent	Ground is less pungent than the root	In brines for meat, fish or seafood. Good for Thai flavours
Juniper	Aromatic and sweet - gin favoured	Whole crushed	Rich, strong, red meat and game
Mace	Strong nutmeg flavour	Ground	Meat and especially sausages
Mixed Spice	A mix of flavours Cinnamon, cloves ginger and allspice	Ground	Rubs and brines for meat and game
Mustard Seed	Slightly hot and warming	Whole or crushed	In brines and pickles. Pork, veal, and rabbit
Nutmeg	Sweet and musky	Ground or freshly grated	Chicken and fish
Onion	Strong	Granulated, ground or crushed	In all brines and marinades
Paprika	Strong, slightly sweet and peppery	Lovely when smoked too! (A layer on a flat dish will cold smoke in less than an hour.)	In brines for fish, shellfish and poultry

Spice	Flavour	Form	Recommended Use
Pepper (use a mix of coloured peppercorns)	Strong, pungent and spicy	Whole or ground	For all fish, meat, game and poultry
Pickling spice	Combination of peppercorns, mustard seeds, cloves, cinnamon, ginger, mace chillies, coriander, allspice	Whole	For a sweet pickle brine for all meat, game or poultry
Poppy seed	Nutty flavour	Whole	In brine for any meat or fish
Saffron	Slightly sweet, strong and brightly coloured yellow	Small strands	Strong yellow colour for fish and rice
Sesame	Nutty, slightly sweet flavour	Whole, crushed or oil	Poultry and all fish
Tamarind	Sweet and sour sharp citrus flavour	Paste or pulp	Meat or fish - use for spicy brines
Turmeric	Strong and bitter	Ground	Fish, poultry, curry, spicy brines
Vanilla	Sweet cocoa flavour	Oils or essence	White meat, poultry and fish

Limit the use of flavours such as celery salt, garlic salt and onion salt in your brine as you will already have enough salt in there

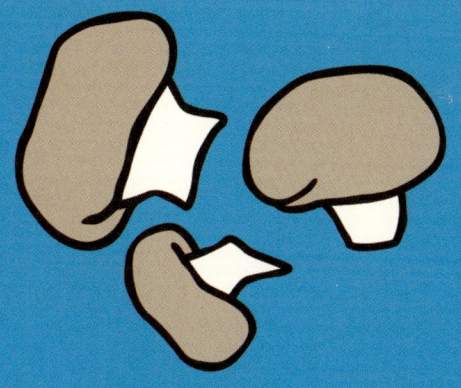

Chapter Eight

Wood

Using wood for smoking

In the old days people would build a pit, start a fire with dry wood and leaves, and then cut off a bough from a tree. They would lay the bough over the fire and, as it was green and full of moisture, it would slowly smoulder, drying out and giving off smoke but little heat. The one thing you never want to see when smoking food is a flame.

Surprisingly, building fires with wood is not that easy! We suggest using another heat source (such as charcoal, a gas ring or electric hot plate) as your main heat source and putting wood on top to create the smoke.

You can use different cuts of woods for different types of smokers. On a Smoky Jo's course we use wood dust, shavings, chips, and logs.

Wood shavings – Dampened wood shavings are mostly used on a heat source such as charcoal or lighted wood logs. Easy to use, easily sourced and cheap, this is a perfect way to produce smoke. Simply dampen the shavings so that when you squeeze a handful and then release it, they form a loose clump in your hand. Place on a wire mesh (such as the grill from an instant BBQ) over the charcoal and, as the shavings get hot, they will begin to smoulder and give off smoke. Be careful when wetting as if they are too wet they will put out the charcoal and if they are too dry they will burst into flames. Just a small distance between the heat source and the damp wood helps to stop the shavings from flaming or putting the heat source out.

> Never put dry wood straight onto heat as it will burst into flames. Make sure if you are putting wood on another heat source that it is damp to ensure it will produce smoke

If you are using an electric or gas heat source, the shavings go on a plate over the heat. They may not need damping in this case – it depends on how close and how hot the heat source is. You may need to experiment.

Damp wood shavings on top of lighted charcoal

Logs – Cutting your wood into small logs is a cost-effective way of smoking. Loose bark and moss, etc should be removed. We use new cut (green) logs or logs that have been soaked overnight. Again, logs are used by putting them on an existing heat source such as burning charcoal or wood. If the wood is seasoned, you will need to soak it overnight or longer to get sufficient moisture into it – without this the logs will simply burst into flame.

Wood chips – Small chips of wood are commercially available and very popular for smoking. We use dampened wood chips on top of hot charcoal or another heat source to create smoke. Chips of the milder woods are fun to use as you can change the flavour by soaking them in your favourite recipe of brine, or in wine, beer, cider or a spirit such as whisky. The chips are often sold as an easy way to do a quick smoke on a BBQ – simply soak a handful of chips in water (or your preferred tipple) and sprinkle them on the hot charcoal to give a smoky flavour whilst barbecuing. I suspect the flavour comes more from the smoke in the air than in the food, but if it's enjoyable, that's fine!

Remember, you NEVER want flames from your fire. You only want smoke

Wood dust – I use wood dust or very small wood chips (2mm) when smoking in a saucepan, a wok, or in the smaller stainless steel boxes such as portable or stovetop smokers. You can also use tea, rice or peat dust in these. The dust needs to be dry and you need only use a small handful. In this situation, the dust is placed inside the box and covered by a drip tray, under the food; the smoker box is put on a heat source. The base gets hot; the wood dust starts to burn and does not burst into flames but chars and starts to smoke, filling the box and smoking the food whilst it cooks. Wood dust can also be used in the same way as dampened wood shavings, if necessary.

Another way to create smoke with wood dust and shavings is to light them directly. They are easier to light than logs or chips, particularly with the assistance of a lighter or small blow torch.

Cold smoke generator

When lit they will gently continue to smoulder for a long time – if you can get the draught just right – giving off smoke and, importantly, very little heat. It is possible to buy a 'cold smoke generator' – a square metal mesh with a spiral design that burns dust over an eight-hour period. A very useful bit of kit!

Getting good quality wood for smoking is imperative. The secret is to try and get wood as natural as you can; this is important to ensure that you only get the wood flavour in the smoke and not all sorts of chemicals which will ruin your best smoking efforts. Most wood that is commercially produced for smoking is now prepared by machines that are lubricated with edible oil.

If using easy lighting charcoal make sure the chemical smell has burnt off before putting it near food

You will use wood shavings in bulk, so try not to pay too much for them. My advice is to cross the palm of a local furniture maker with a smoked sausage or two and negotiate a deal to buy his hard-wood shavings. Make sure they understand the need for hard wood only – you don't want highly resinous pine or worse, processed MDF! It has happened... Dust and chips can seem expensive but it is worth paying for quality and even a small 500 gms bag will last for quite a few smokings.

What wood can I use?

Although woods for smoking food over are commercially available, foraging or bartering can be more rewarding! What woods you use then depends on where you are and what is available. Smoking should always be done over hard wood such as oak or beech. In America, hickory is a firm favourite and particularly in the Deep South they go for much stronger woods such as mesquite. In some Scandinavian countries and other European areas, people may smoke over softer woods such as pines. I would suggest that these are avoided – they have a higher tar content, tend to flame at lower temperatures than hard woods and carry a strong resinous flavour that is not to everyone's palate.

Fruit trees such as apple, cherry, pear and damson are very good to smoke over. I went foraging last year when storms caused damage to some of the damson orchards in the Lyth Valley in the south of Cumbria. The results of smoking over damson wood – especially red meats – have been mouth-watering.

Here is yet another opportunity to flavour your food! You can add your own recipes of herbs and spices in with the wood dust or shavings, or simply sprinkle herbs and spices onto the dampened wood.

Woods to be wary of...

Pines, firs and any soft pithy woods such as elderberry should be avoided, and any wood with a very strong 'gum/resin' smell (such as cedar, cypress or eucalyptus) is unsuitable for smoking. Yew, horse chestnut (conker) and laburnum may be toxic. (Research from the internet, and I'm not minded to try and prove it wrong!)

Be careful where you get your wood from. Avoid sourcing from saw mills as they cut the wood on machines that are lubricated with industrial lubricants and these will taint the taste of your food. As previously mentioned, wood turners and furniture makers are a good source of hard woods.

Also avoid buying wood scraps as you will not know what is in them and they are likely to contain pine, shavings of MDF and wood that may have been painted, stained, glued or treated in some way – all of which will taint the taste of your food and may give off toxins when burned.

There is much written about different woods and the different flavours they impart. The table on the next page lists a few of the most popular woods that you can use and some ideas of which foods they complement:

Wood	Flavour	Food
Oak	Oak is probably the most common wood used in food smoking in the UK. It has a very mild taste and allows the brine flavours to come though. Gives food a great colour.	All fish, meat, poultry, game, vegetables, nuts and fruits. Use oak for any type of smoking.
Beech	Like oak, this is commonly used for smoking. It is very mild, has a lovely gentle aroma.	Great for smoking all types of food but especially good with salmon, shellfish and fruit.
Ash	Not so often used but is a good wood to smoke over.	Ash has quite a distinctive flavour. Good with all red meat and game.
Hazel	This is a new wood to the art of smoking and is proving to be very popular. A very mild wood, allowing the flavour of the food and brines to come through.	Poultry, fish, ham and vegetables. Good with olives, cheese and shellfish.
Sweet Chestnut	This wood produces a slightly sweet and nutty flavour.	Good with all meats.
Apple	A lovely wood for smoking with a slightly sweet flavour.	Ham, beef, pork, pheasant and poultry. Popular for smoking cheese.
Cherry	A sweet and fruity flavoured wood with a colouring element that turns food golden.	All meat and game.
Pear	A mild sweet flavour.	Good with poultry, cheese and pork.
Damson	A lovely sweet almost treacly flavour!	Lovely with ham and chicken.
Peach	Mild and sweet with a woody flavour.	Poultry and pork.
Crab Apple	A deep fruity flavour.	Good with poultry and lamb.
Hickory	Very popular in the USA. A strong deep flavour. It produces dark colour. Does not grow naturally in the UK but is available via the internet.	Good with all meat and venison particularly beef and ribs.
Mesquite	Again popular in the USA. A strong woody somewhat earthy flavour but with a sweet undertone. Does not grow naturally in the UK but is available via the internet.	All meat, game, poultry and vegetables.
Maple	Sweet with a subtle smoky flavour.	A favourite for all poultry. Good for fish, cheese and vegetables.

What else can I smoke over?

There are three other substances that will create smoke without bursting into flames: rice, tea and peat.

Rice – Dry uncooked rice will burn in the same way as wood dust, smouldering gently giving off smoke. You can either use the rice as a sort of heat source and place herbs and spices on top of it to create different flavours, or you can use flavoured rice. Just burning plain uncooked rice on its own can produce a bitter taste in your food.

Tea – Use the best grade tea leaves that you can get. Again, tea leaves will behave in the same way as wood dust, smouldering gently and giving off wonderful flavoured smoke. Have fun trying out the different flavours of your favourite teas. Do not use tea that has come from a tea bag as the quality will not be good; it will be more dust than leaf and, if it is a fruit tea, it may have been the bag that was impregnated with the smell and flavour, not the leaf.

Peat – Smoking over peat gives your food a wonderful dark colour, with a strong, distinctive smell and taste. You can either use peat dust in exactly the same way you would use wood dust, or you can buy sacks of peat blocks which are simply blocks of dried peat. Depending on the texture, they can be used in the same way as you would use a seasoned wood log, or can be 'grated' to create shavings. I would buy peat for smoking rather than 'gather' it, as you ideally need peat from hard-wood areas. Peat from soft wood areas can be acrid.

Other – The joy of food smoking is that people are always coming up with new ideas of how to smoke and what to smoke over. In vogue at the moment is smoking in hay – tomorrow it will be something else – so go on, experiment you could come up with the next good new idea.

Chapter Nine

Smokers

As we explained in Chapter 3, there are a number of ways you can smoke food. In addition, there are a huge number of containers in which you can smoke. At Smoky Jo's we are always inventing new ways of smoking – from our first smoker, Freddie the filing cabinet, to smoking in a clay oven and in a wardrobe! However, there are some excellent commercially produced smokers out there and I use a selection of them on our smoking courses.

The main point of this chapter is to help you get started with the process of fires, creating smoke, and hot and cold smoking in whatever type of smoker you have decided to buy or build.

Barrel smokers

This is a classic barrel smoker – they come in all sorts of shapes and sizes, some quite small and other looking like Stevenson's Rocket! However, the principle of them all is the same. The one we use at Smoky Jo's comes in two sizes and is produced by Landmann. It is ideal for home smoking, being light and portable, and can be used as a cold smoker, a hot smoker and a BBQ. Why I particularly like this design is that it has a chimney at the side and not in the top; this stops the problem of condensation dripping on your food which can occur if you smoke on cold days.

© **Image courtesy of Landmann**

The small offset chamber on the left is the fire box. The main chamber is where you put the food. It has a door on the side of the fire box and a chimney with a lid at the end of the food box for regulating the draught. It has an excellent thermometer in the lid, a useful wooden shelf and wheels.

Light a fire in the fire box. I suggest that for ease you use a disposable BBQ or loose charcoal with a mesh over the top and place clumps of dampened wood shavings or small damp logs on top of the mesh to create the smoke.

For hot smoking, build a big fire in the fire box, add a damp log or two, close the lids and leave to smoke and get hot for a number of hours, leaving your food to cook slowly over a low heat. Do not open the food chamber as this causes a loss of heat.

A thermometer with a remote probe is ideal for hot smoking! Alternatively, after cold smoking you can put charcoal under the food on the BBQ grill and BBQ your food while still smoking it.

For cold smoking, build a small fire in the same way and leave to smoke. This is ideal if you are then going to hot smoke your food after cold smoking it. If you are just cold smoking, be mindful of the temperature. Alternatively you can use a cold smoke generator in the fire box.

Cold smoke generator

This amazing little gizmo is produced by ProQ smokers. It has revolutionised home smoking. With this bit of kit you can produce smoke for up to 10 hours without generating any heat. This means that you can even cold smoke in a cardboard box. ProQ have brought out a cardboard Eco Smoker designed for just that purpose.

This is a fantastic smoker – and a personal favourite – simply fill the Eco Smoker with food; fill the cold smoke generator with fine wood dust, light it with the tea light provided, when the dust has caught, remove the tea light and place on the metal tray at the bottom of the Eco Smoker. The smoke will then slowly burn away for about ten hours gently smoking your food. I love this smoker, it takes all the hard work out of cold smoking and it needs very little attention once the wood is burning. In addition, pop this gizmo into the bottom of any vented hot smoker and you can turn it into a cold smoker.

We smoke everything in this smoker from butter and scallops to salmon and water; everything gets cold smoked and anything that then requires cooking gets popped in the Aga – what could be easier?

A couple of points to make about this smoker – it is great for a smoker or

73

© Image courtesy of MacsBBQ

chamber the size of the Eco Smoker but I do not think it generates enough smoke for a chamber that is much bigger than the Eco Smoker. So if you have a water smoker or barrel smoker or anything with the capacity similar to a 40 gallon size drum or a small fridge I suggest that you use the Cold Smoke Generator's big brother – The Artisan. The Artisan is exactly the same as the Cold Smoke Generator only it is three times the size and also gives off about three times the smoke and will smoke away for about 16 hours.

Secondly if you are going to use either of these smokers in any chamber other than the Eco Smoker (the Artisan is not suitable for the Eco Smoker) please make sure that you place them on a metal tray or surface inside your smoker and remember to take the tea light out!

Water smoker

ProQ also have their own range of smokers, a number of which are water smokers. Water smokers have a base for the fire, a bowl for water or liquid above the fire and racks for placing the food on and/or hooks for hanging the food. They come with an accurate thermometer in the lid. They are excellent hot smokers, cooking the food slowly at a low temperature. The addition of water helps to control the temperature and keeps the food moist as it creates what is almost a steamy smoke.

Traditionally water smokers have only been hot smokers, as it can be hard to smoke in them and keep temperatures below 25–30°C. However, with the introduction of The Artisan, cold smoking is easy in a water smoker. Simply place the lighted cold smoke generator in the base, place or hang the food in the chamber and cold smoke.

© Image courtesy of MacsBBQ

To hot smoke, I again suggest the use of charcoal as a heat source – once sealed inside it burns slowly – and then place soaked or green logs on top to create your smoke. You can put herbs and spices in the water bowl or you can use other liquids such as wine, beer or cider ... though I prefer mine in a glass!

Once your charcoal is red hot (a charcoal chimney is ideal for this), add your wood, place the food in the smoker and shut the smoker. Put the top on and LEAVE IT! This is a slow process – every time you take the lid off the smoker you will prolong the smoking process by at least 20 minutes. So be patient and you will be rewarded with the most succulent and delicious food. As a guide, sausages should take about 1 hour; whole chickens should take about 3–4 hours, and a gammon joint or rolled shoulder of lamb about 6–8 hours. Probe the food with a thermometer to ensure it is cooked; one with a probe you can leave in the meat with the gauge on the outside is perfect. For cooking guide see page 89.

Stovetop smoker

Below is a Cameron stovetop hot-smoker. These come in two sizes and their great value is that they can go on any heat source. Whatever type of stove you have in your kitchen, whether Aga, gas, or electric, you can use this to smoke in. In addition, they will also go on any outside wood fire, gas or charcoal BBQ.

Simply put a small handful of dry small wood chips, wood or peat dust (or your own smoking mixture using things like tea, herbs, rice and sugar) in the base of the pan. Cover it with the drip tray and rack. Place the food on the rack. Put it on a high heat with the lid half on. As soon as you see a whiff of smoke, turn the heat down slightly, shut the lid and leave it. As the smoking mix gets hot it will begin to char and give off smoke, filling the box with smoke. As the smoke burns away and is absorbed, the box simply cooks the food. You will be amazed at how little smoke escapes.

© **Image courtesy of CookEquip**

Portable smoker

The portable – or riverside – hot smoker works in exactly the same way as the stovetop smoker, only it comes with its own heat source. The smoker sits securely on a base that holds two small burners which, when filled with methylated spirit, will burn for 30–35 minutes.

Again use a handful of dry small wood chip, wood or peat dust, tea or rice in the base of the pan. Cover it with the drip plate, put the food on the racks and put the lid on. Light the burners and put the box on the base.

I use this little smoker when I am fishing, and the first trout caught gets killed, gutted and hot smoked all within about 12 minutes! (This makes a fantastic breakfast; sometimes a lunch, but often I don't get to eat until much later in the day!)

Electric smoker

This is a Bradley smoker; it is electric and takes all the hassle out of smoking. There is no need to light fires or create smoke, so it is clean and efficient.

© Image courtesy of Bradley Smokers

For hot smoking you simply plug it in, load it with food, load it with Bradley's own bisquettes and turn it on. The bisquettes move down the chute and along inside the smoking chamber over a heated plate. They heat up and start to smoulder, giving off smoke. As they burn away, the machine replenishes the bisquettes, which are available in eleven different flavours.

For cold smoking you can buy a cold smoke adaptor to go with it that simply plugs into the side.

Using an electric smoker is an easy way to smoke food. It produces a consistent product and is therefore an ideal smoker for anyone who is thinking of going into smoking on a commercial basis to try out their products on a small scale.

Gas Smoker

There are now similar smokers to the electric smoker on the market but are powered by Calor gas. These are particularly useful for those people smoking outside in a shed or barn that may not have an electricity supply. They work on a very similar system and can be used to both hot and cold smoke.

Ceramic Smokers

The Big Green Egg is the best known of these smokers – smoking and cooking in a unique way. These are wonderful inventions and those people lucky enough to own one are completely addicted to them! They are one of the more expensive smokers on the market and can be used for smoking, grilling and as a BBQ. There are also an increasing number of other ceramic designed smokers available made by different companies – so lots to choose from.

Accessories

For those who like gadgets there are also instruments available that will manage the ventilation in your smoker to ensure a steady temperature, quite often accompanied by an App so you can monitor your smoker from your mobile phone! At smoky Jo's we are still happy with opening the wardrobe door!

Just for good measure, here is how we use some of our home-designed smokers.

Freddie!

OK, so here are Smoky Jo and Smoky Georgina in human form (I know, the cartoons are better!) with our first-ever home smoker, Freddie. These make great cold smokers. It's easy to convert: simply drill a few holes in the front of the base and in the front of the bottom drawer, then drill a few holes in the base of each drawer and cut a hole in the top for a chimney.
I light a fire in the bottom drawer, using either a disposable BBQ or loose charcoal in a disposable BBQ tray or metal dish, then cover it with a mesh and place damp wood shavings on top to create the smoke. We do this without food first, to 'cure' the cabinet.

Image courtesy of Cumbria Life magazine

When smoking, fill all three of the remaining drawers with food. If you are going to hot smoke any food after the cold smoking, make sure you put that food in the bottom drawer where the temperature can get a little warm for cold smoking. You can use the bottom drawer for nuts if you like them warmed through, or there is usually sufficient heat to slowly hot smoke raw shellfish!

If I am firing up Freddie, I fill all the drawers with food to smoke – salmon, cheese, duck, chicken, nuts, olives, prawns – you name it! Anything that then needs hot smoking or cooking, like the duck and chicken, either goes in my

water smoker to be hot smoked, or gets cooked in the Aga in the conventional way, or goes in the freezer to be cooked another day. Don't let anything raw that needs cooking drip on anything that is not going to be cooked!

Wardrobe smoker

Here we have our wardrobe smoker – this has been designed exactly on the basis of my first diagram. I have used an old wood-burning stove, a length of chimney liner and an old wardrobe with a hole cut out in the top for a chimney. I light a fire in the wood burner with charcoal, put damp wood shavings or damp logs on top to generate the smoke, and this is piped through to the wardrobe where the food is either hanging or on racks. If I am only smoking a small amount of food, I will simply use The Artisan in the bottom of the wardrobe. As a note – if you use charcoal as your heat source, you can use lump wood or briquettes. Be careful not to use any charcoal that offers itself as 'easy or instant lighting' as this will have been impregnated with flammable liquid which will taint the taste of your food. If you do use this, make sure the smell of the starter has burned away before you put your wood on and start smoking.

Smoky Jo's wardrobe cold smoker - see diagram on Page 30

If you are using a disposable BBQ, make sure that the impregnated sheet has burnt well away and that the charcoal is all white before you use it. This is to ensure that any chemicals on the sheet have evaporated and will not taint the taste of your food.

I have found English-made charcoal, any restaurant-grade charcoal or charcoal made from coconut husks to be excellent, although the latter tends to burn at a higher temperature.

If you do not want to use charcoal as your heat source, you can try to light your wood directly but this inevitably runs the risk of creating a flame — which you do not want.

You can also try lighting dry wood dust directly, either in a heap, or spread a trail of dust in a spiral shape and light one end. This should smoulder away for a few hours, if you get the draught just right, creating smoke but no flame.

Chapter Ten

And so to smoking!

This chapter aims to show you how to smoke your food in a traditional way. Remember the three diagrams:

Cold smoking – Salt, rinse and dry, then cold smoke for a long time.
Hot smoking (cold smoking first) – Salt, rinse and dry, cold smoke for a few hours, then hot smoke.
Hot smoking (without first cold smoking) – Salt, rinse and put straight into a hot smoker.

Unless stated, all food can be prepared in the same way. Choose your brine solution and create your recipe by adding herbs and spices. You can use an ice-cream tub, jug, bucket or bag. We often use strong self-sealing bags, but never assume they will stay standing up and sealed – that can lead to large brine puddles! Stainless steel should be OK but be aware that salt water can occasionally corrode cheaper pans. There should be enough brine for the food to swim about a bit, were it likely to do that! Place food in the brine and ensure that it is fully submerged (you may need to put a plate or similar on top of the food to keep it under the liquid) and leave. Once brined for the required amount of time, take the food out and rinse it under cold running water and dry before smoking it.

Suggested brining and smoking times

These are suggestions, and calculated for home cooking that will be either eaten within a few days or frozen (i.e. treated like any other cooked meat or fish). Additionally, these recipes do not take account of your unique taste buds! The preparation and smoking of food are completely open to your own likes and dislikes. There are few hard and fast rules.

I would suggest that you start with a low-percentage brine solution. The recipes given use a medium brine solution. This is a good starting point for your smoking experimentation; the food will not be too salty or too smoky, and the texture will not be changed dramatically. (Many people have been put off eating smoked chicken by mass-produced food that has been over-salted, leading to a rubbery texture.) If you prefer a stronger smoky flavour there are several ways to achieve this: you can increase the percentage of salt solution; you can keep the same strength but brine it for longer, or you can smoke the food for longer. Remember, the longer the food is in the brine, the more salt it will absorb. The more salt absorbed by the food, the more concentrated the flavours, and the more the smoke will penetrate it and deepen the smoky flavour.

Brining and smoking times – This is only a guide. You will need to experiment to get the flavour to suit your palate. Recommended smoking times are a suggested minimum for food that is going to be cold smoked then cooked in an oven. The times can therefore be used as a guide for food to be cold then hot smoked.

Food	Brine for	Smoke for
Whole chicken	24 hours	6 hours
Chicken crowns	12 hours	4 hours
Chicken fillet	3 hours	2 hours
Guinea fowl	12 hours	6 hours
Whole duck	12 hours	6 hours
Duck fillet	3 hours	2 hours
Whole goose	24 hours	8 hours
Goose fillet	3 - 5 hours	3 hours
Whole turkey	24 - 36 hours	12 hours
Pheasant	12 hours	3 hours
Quail	10 hours	4 hours
Pigeon breast	4 hours	1 hour
Rabbit/hare	12 hours	6 hours
Rolled shoulder of lamb	24 hours	6 hours

Food	Brine for	Smoke for
Mutton (1 kg)	24 hours	8 hours
Large joint (2 kg+) of beef, venison, pork, lamb	12 hours per kg	6 hours
Large joint (2 kg+) of beef, venison, lamb for cold smoking	12 hours per kg	24 hours
Steak	20 min (rub)	1 hour
Beef mince	1 hr (seasoning)	1 hour
Brisket	12 hours (rub)	6 hours
Pork fillet	12 hours	6 hours
Bacon joint	N/A	12 hours
Sausages	N/A	2 hours
Gammon (soak first)	N/A	8 hours
Trout (175 - 400 gms)	30 - 60 mins	2 hours
Side of salmon for cold smoking 1 - 2 kg	8 - 10 hours	10 hours
Salmon fillets for hot smoking	30 - 45 mins	2 hours
Raw shellfish - prawns, scallops	2 - 5 mins	2 hours
Cooked shellfish	N/A	1 hour
Squid and octopus	5 - 30 mins	3 hours
Kippers	30 mins	5 hours
Mackerel	1 hour	2 hours
Smokies	30 - 45 mins	2 hours
Haddock	30 - 45 mins	3 hours
Whitebait	5 - 10 mins	3 hours
Tuna steaks	30 - 45 mins	1 hour
Fish roe	1 - 5 mins	6 hours
Hens' eggs	10 mins	6 hours
Cheeses	N/A	6 hours

Dry salting for cold smoked fish

Food	Salt for	Smoke for
Whole side of farmed salmon 1 - 2 kg	8 - 10 hours	10 hours
Whole sides of wild salmon 1 - 2 kg	4 - 5 hours	10 hours
Whole tuna loins	10 hours	24 hours
Halibut	4 - 6 hours	8 hours

Fruit, vegetables and other foods

Food	Brine for	Smoke for
Garlic bulb	N/A	24 hours
Onions	N/A	6 hours
Peppers	N/A	3 hours
Tomatoes	N/A	20 - 30 minutes
Mushrooms	N/A	2 hours
Apples	N/A	4 hours
Oranges	N/A	6 hours
Bananas	N/A	4 hours
Damson	N/A	4 hours
Berries	N/A	2 hours
Olives	N/A	2 hours
Nuts	N/A	4 hours
Tofu	N/A	6 - 8 hours
Quorn	N/A	4 - 6 hours
Flour	N/A	4 - 6 hours
Salt	N/A	6 - 8 hours
Sugar	N/A	6 - 8 hours
Herbs and Spice	N/A	2 - 4 hours
Pulses and Beans	N/A	2 - 4 hours
Seeds and Grains	N/A	2 - 4 hours
Syrups	N/A	2 - 6 hours
Butter	N/A	4 - 8 hours
Cream	N/A	2 - 4 hours
Oils	N/A	6 - 10 hours
Vinegars	N/A	6 - 10 hours
Hummus	N/A	4 - 6 hours
Gnocchi	N/A	3 - 4 hours
Packets and Mixes	N/A	2 - 3 hours
Water	N/A	2 - 6 hours
Vodka and other spirits	N/A	2 - 4 hours
Avocado	N/A	10 - 20 minutes
Mangos	N/A	5 - 10 minutes

Fruit, vegetables and other foods

Food	Brine for	Smoke for
Chocolate	N/A	20 - 30 minutes
Marshmallows	N/A	10 minutes
Root vegetables	N/A	3 - 5 hours
Chillis	N/A	4 - 6 hours
Asparagus	N/A	30 minutes
Coffee	N/A	30 minutes
Marrow	30 minutes	1 - 1$\frac{1}{2}$ hours
Lemons	N/A	1 - 2 hours
Apricots	N/A	1 hour
Grapes	N/A	30 minutes
Dried fruit	N/A	1 hour
Soft fruit	N/A	1 hour

All smoking times are approximate and meant as a guide. My suggestion with everything in this section is to smoke the food for the lowest recommended time, and then taste it – if you want it smokier put it back in to smoke or if it is too smoky for you, you will know to reduce the smoking time next time.

Some books I have read state that you can re-use your brines; you will know when it can no longer be used because it starts to smell 'sour'. I never re-use a brine. I fear that having a bucket of used brine standing can be risky, and obviously its salinity goes down when you use it! For the sake of a few pennies I would always use fresh brine.

Important tips to remember before you start:

- If the food is to be cold smoked then after brining, either leave it to dry overnight or dry it off with a paper towel before placing it in the cold smoker.
- If the food is going straight into a hot smoker, then it is less important to have it dry before it is placed in the smoker.
- If you are cold smoking and then hot smoking food, remember that in order to prevent the food from becoming dried out by the heat and becoming tough, cook it low and slow for a long time at a low temperature.

ε• If you are smoking (particularly cold smoking) a large piece of meat or one that has a thick covering of fat, you will need to brine it and smoke it for a longer time to ensure that the smoke has time to fully penetrate the flesh and for the food to dry out.

ε• If you over-salt your food for any reason, do not panic. Simply put it in cold water to soak and the salt will come out – in other words, osmosis will occur again. This time the salt in the food will move to the unsalted water around it, re-hydrating the food.

ε• Smoking times are approximate and you will refine these as you become more practised and develop your own recipes, brining and cooking times. Depending on how smoky and salty you like your food, you can either use a stronger salt solution in your brine, or brine the food for a longer time, or you can cold smoke it for longer.

ε• Remember, if you are cold smoking you need to ensure the food has lost the required amount of weight. If you are going to hot smoke or cook the food this weight loss is not relevant; what is important is that it is sufficiently cooked to be safe to eat – see below.

ε• In ordinary ovens we tend to cook at high temperatures for a short time. Smoked food should ideally be cooked for a longer time at a low temperature. To ensure the food is fully cooked through, the easiest way is to probe it with a thermometer. You are looking for not only the temperature it has reached but also how long it has been at that temperature.

ε• If the food you are using has been previously frozen, you must reduce the salting time. The freezing process breaks down the cells of the food and this allows the salt to penetrate the cells more easily. This means that your food absorbs the salt quicker and it can taste too salty.

Cooking guidelines

These are times and core temperatures required when cooking meat to kill E coli 0157, Salmonella and Listeria:

ε• 60°C for 45 minutes, or
ε• 65°C for 10 minutes, or
ε• 70°C for 2 minutes, or
ε• 75°C for 30 seconds, or
ε• 80°C for 6 seconds.

If in doubt cook for longer and always make sure your food is piping hot before serving – but make sure that you do not dry out the food with the heat! Some foods may look more 'raw' than you are used to – red juices – but think 'sous-vide'. This cooking method is designed to use a low temperature, e.g. 60°C, for as long as 72 hours to cook a large piece of food evenly through without losing many of its 'raw' qualities.

Always make sure that you use the very best quality food to smoke. You cannot make a silk purse out of a sow's ear!

Poultry

Poultry smokes well and, if your preparation is done right, the flesh should be succulent, moist and of course delicious. For safety reasons, you would never eat cold smoked poultry. All poultry should be either hot smoked or cooked after being cold smoked.

Once cooked through, all hot smoked poultry can be served either cold or hot. If you are going to re-heat it, wrap it in foil with a spoonful of liquid (water or wine, etc) and loosely wrap it to form a parcel. Warm it slowly in the oven. The liquid will stop it drying out. Ensure it is piping hot before serving.

Chicken

One important point about smoking poultry is to try to use 'skin-on' meat. This is becoming harder and harder to buy but it is important because, although the smoking process dries the food, we don't want the flesh to become tough and dry. The skin helps to keep the flesh tender.

You can smoke all or part of a chicken: the breast, thighs, wings or the whole bird. If smoking a whole bird, ensure that the inside of the bird is clean and rinsed before brining. Brine the chicken in your own recipe for 24 hours for a whole bird, 12 hours for a crown and 3 hours for chicken fillets or pieces. After brining, rinse off the bird and then allow to drip-dry. After drying, I brush the meat with a little vegetable oil just to help it keep tender through the drying process.

At this point you can reinforce the flavour of your brine recipe by sprinkling a flavour on the skin. For example, if I have brined my chicken in my favourite recipe (see page 50) using white wine and tarragon, I would just sprinkle a few pieces of chopped tarragon over the skin before I put it in the smoker. I would not introduce any new flavours at this stage but use the main ingredient of the brine to help reinforce the flavour, although that is personal preference. At the Old Smokehouse, one of our most popular products was chicken fillet salted in a sweet pickle brine then oiled and seasoned with Cajun spices.

Put a whole chicken in the cold smoker and cold smoke it for 6–8 hours (4 hours for a crown) and then hot smoke or cook. This can be done by increasing the temperature in the cold smoker or moving the chicken to a hot smoker until the food is cooked. An alternative is to cook it in a conventional way in an oven.

Chicken fillets and thighs will only need 2 hours cold smoking, then hot smoke slowly or cook in an oven.

When smoking poultry always try to get meat with skin on. This will help to keep the flesh moist

Guinea fowl
Smoke in the same way as a whole chicken. Brine in your own recipe brine for 12 hours and then rinse thoroughly and allow to drip-dry. Cold smoke for 6–8 hours. The flesh of guinea fowl has a tendency to dry out, so ensure you cook it slowly at a low temperature. Hot smoke slowly or cook in an oven.

Duck
There are few foods as delicious as smoked duck. Smoke in the same way as chicken – either whole or fillets – but ensure that you cook the fillets very gently at a low temperature. It should be served pink. This will ensure that it is moist and succulent. Brine a whole duck in your own recipe brine for 12 hours (3 hours for a fillet) and then rinse thoroughly and dry. Cold smoke a whole bird for 6–8 hours and a fillet for 2–3 hours. Hot smoke slowly or cook in an oven. Serve it cold or re-heated. (Although it can be reheated gently in a foil parcel, with duck I prefer to put it skin-side down on a hot pan to crisp the skin up!)

Goose
Well, perhaps there is one thing more delicious then smoked duck: smoked goose breast. Again, smoke in the same way as chicken or duck but, depending

on the size, you will need to brine it and smoke it for longer. Brine in your own recipe brine for 24 hours (3 hours for a goose breast) and then rinse. Allow to drip-dry overnight. Depending on the size, cold smoke between 8–24 hours (3 hours for a breast). Hot smoke slowly or cook in an oven. Serve it hot or cold.

Turkey

Turkey is a much maligned meat, in spite of Norfolk's best efforts! We tend to eat it only for high days and holidays then complain, but actually it is available all year round and is relatively inexpensive. It is also a healthy option, being lower in fat and cholesterol than some other meat – and it smokes absolutely beautifully!

Treat a small turkey the same as a goose, but if you are dealing with a bird over 3 kg you will need to brine it for longer. Brine in your own recipe brine for 24–36 hours and then rinse it thoroughly. Allow it to drip-dry. Cold smoke a large bird for at least 12–16 hours, and 24 hours for a really large bird. Hot smoke slowly or cook in an oven. Serve hot or cold.

Turkey crowns and thighs can be smoked the same as whole chicken.

Quail

This small compact bird is a real delicacy when smoked. Despite its tiny size, it takes a long time to take on the brine and the smoke. Brine in your own recipe brine for 10 hours, then rinse thoroughly and let it drip-dry before putting it in the cold smoker for 4–6 hours. Then hot smoke or cook slowly in an oven. Normally served cold.

Game

I am concentrating on venison, rabbit and pheasant in this section although many people will be smoking other food such as wild goose, wild duck, partridge, etc – most of which are covered elsewhere in this chapter. It is worth noting the animals reared in the wild are generally less fatty than commercially reared animals and so will require less brining time.

Venison

Venison can be either hot or cold smoked. Both are delicious but of course cold smoking takes much longer, and you may need to have the facility to air dry the meat after cold smoking.

Cold smoked venison

Weigh the joint. This is very important as you will need to be sure that it has lost 25% of its weight to ensure that it is safe to eat.

Brine in your own recipe brine and, depending on the size of the piece of meat, you should brine it for between 12–36 hours – 12 hours per 1 kg. Rinse and dry. Oil the flesh with vegetable oil and then cold smoke for 24–36 hours, ideally in an environment with good airflow. This should eliminate the need for further drying. Smoke at a temperature below 25°C. If the temperature rises over 30°C, your venison will start to cook.

Weigh the joint. If it has not lost its 25% of weight you can do one of two things. Firstly, you can light another fire and cold smoke it for longer. The risk in this is that you might end up with food that is too smoky. The alternative is to have some way of air drying the meat. This will help it to lose the required weight without increasing the smoky flavour.

There are a number of effective ways you can air dry meat or fish, all of which I have tried. You can:

- Rig up a fan in your smoker.
- Put the meat under an ordinary desk fan for a few hours.
- Put the meat in a fan oven WITHOUT the heat on for a few hours.
- Use a room dehumidifier in a larder overnight.
- Build some sort of air-drying chamber where you can put the meat to air-dry.

I have had great success with an old fridge that I have converted. I removed the motor but kept the inside racks. I cut one hole in the back and another in the top and covered them with very fine copper gauze to allow the air to flow through but keep the dust out. I then rigged up an old blade fan from an extractor fan in the bottom and made a hole in the side for the cable. In this, I place any food that has taken on enough smoke but has not lost sufficient moisture to be safe to eat. I have found that after a few hours in this air dryer, the food has reached its desirable weight and is safe to eat.

You will find that you will not need to air dry cold smoked food so much in the summer — except when it is very humid (not often a problem here in Shap!) — as your smoker will do the job well. On very damp wet days, or through the winter, a means of air drying may be essential. A purpose built air-drying chamber will also be a useful bit of kit if you enjoy making your own biltong or jerky, or it can be used in other curing processes.

Once your venison has lost its required weight it is ready to eat. It is easier to slice after an hour in the freezer.

It is easier to slice cold smoked fish and meat if it has been in the freezer for an hour or so

Hot smoked venison

This is the more usual way to smoke venison. Salt in your chosen recipe brine; depending on the size of the piece of meat you should brine it for 12 hours per 1 kg of meat. Rinse and dry. Oil the flesh with vegetable oil and then cold smoke for 10–12 hours. Hot smoke slowly or cook in an oven. Serve it cold or re-heated.

Rabbit

Rabbit is a very lean meat. Keep this in mind when smoking; you don't want it to dry too much or it may be tough. Brine in your own recipe brine for 12 hours. Rinse off and dry and then brush all over with oil. This will help to keep it moist. Cold smoke for 6–8 hours and then hot smoke or gently cook in an oven. Best served hot, or added to a game stew.

Hare

Similar to rabbit and can be smoked in the same way.

Pheasant

Pheasant has very little fat so I always cover the flesh with streaky bacon before smoking. Treat the same way as chicken. Brine in your own recipe brine for 12 hours and then rinse thoroughly. Let the whole bird drip-dry before covering in bacon and putting it in the cold smoker. Cold smoke for 3–6 hours. Hot smoke slowly or cook in an oven. The thin strips of bacon get too smoky for most people, so remove before carving, although Ollie, who came on a smoking course and devoured it with delight, saying 'Wonderful! It's like eating a bonfire!' As I have said, smoked food is all about personal taste...

Pheasant is so easily available these days that many people just take the breast to eat. These need to be brined for 1–2 hours, wrapped in streaky bacon, cold smoked for two hours and then gently hot smoked or cooked in an oven. Serve it cold or re-heated.

Pigeon breast

Smoke pigeon breast the same way as pheasant breast. Brine in your own recipe brine for 4 hours, dry and then rinse. Cold smoke for 1–2 hours, then hot smoke or cook. Wrap in foil instead of bacon if cooking in an oven. Serve it cold or re-heated.

Meat

As a general guide, any meat you enjoy cooked rare you can eat cold smoked – beef, venison and lamb, for example. Eating uncooked pork is only done after more intensive curing, such as for Parma ham and prosciutto. So always cook or hot smoke pork.

Pork

The smoking process for pork is the same as for all meat, game and poultry. Brine the meat in your own recipe for 12 hours per 1 kg. Rinse and dry and ideally let it mature for 24 hours. Brush with oil and cold smoke it for 10–12 hours then hot smoke or cook gently in an oven.

Pork fillet

Smoked pork fillet is lean and quite delicate. Brine it in your own recipe for 12 hours for a whole fillet, rinse and dry, then leave to mature for 12 hours. Brush with oil before cold smoking for 6–8 hours and then hot smoking or gently cooking in an oven.

Gammon

A gammon is an uncooked ham; the thigh and rump of a pig that has been cured. Unlike virtually everything else in this book, where we suggest that you brine before smoking, a gammon is different. Having already been cured with salt, it normally needs only to be soaked before you smoke it. As it already has a lot of salt in the flesh, it attracts a lot of smoke. So if you don't soak it before smoking it tends to come out a little too salty and maybe too smoky in flavour.

Unless you love food the taste of bonfire, I suggest that a gammon joint should be soaked overnight, rinsed and dried, brushed with oil and cold smoked for 8–10 hours before being hot smoked or cooked in an oven.

Using a food thermometer with a remote probe is ideal when smoking food

Pulled pork

This is very much an American delicacy and there are many recipes from the different Southern States. It is delicious and is normally served with a rich BBQ sauce.

Rather than a brine, a 'rub' (a mix of salt and spices) is usually used. Cover the pork joint – normally a boned shoulder – with a rub of your own recipe. Place in a plastic or marinating bag and refrigerate overnight. Do not rinse. Place the joint in a cold smoker and smoke for 4–6 hours. Remove from the smoker and place on a double layer of foil. Pour over a BBQ sauce, seal the foil parcel and cook at a low heat for 8–10 hours. Remove from oven and serve – the pork should be so tender that you can cut it with a spoon!

Bacon

You can cure your own bacon or buy an unsliced piece from your butcher. Simply put it in a cold smoker for 10–12 hours, then slice and grill or fry.

Beef

Beef is wonderful either hot or cold smoked. The leaner cuts are preferable. I have always found topside or silverside to be the best to smoke. However steaks – sirloin, rump or fillet – are amazing smoked before frying or grilling. Then, of course, there is American-style smoked brisket.

Hot smoked beef

Brine in a sweet-pickle base brine with your own added ingredients. Brine the meat for 12 hours per 1 kg of meat. Rinse and allow to dry overnight. Brush with vegetable oil and place in a cold smoker for 8–10 hours or more. Then hot smoke or gently cook in an oven. Serve hot or cold.

Cold smoked beef

The whole process of just cold smoking takes much longer than hot smoking. Allowing the meat to rest and mature for a few hours during the different stages of the process can be very beneficial.

Weigh the meat; this is important as you need to achieve at least 25% weight loss for the meat to be safe to eat.

Brine in a sweet-pickle brine with your own added ingredients. (Our favourite addition is crushed juniper berries.) Brine the meat for 12 hours per kilo of meat. Rinse and drip-dry and allow to mature for 24 hours. Brush with oil and place in a cold smoker for at least 24–36 hours and smoke at a temperature below 25°C. If the temperature rises over 30°C, the beef will start to cook and may spoil. Weigh the meat. It is ready when it has lost 25% of its weight. If it has not lost its weight after this time, see cold smoked venison for further details about air drying on page 95.

Steak
Sprinkle salt, sugar and pepper (plus herbs or spices if you wish) on both sides of the steak and then tenderise with a tenderising hammer. Leave for 20 minutes. Brush with oil and place in cold smoker for one hour. Either hot smoke slowly to taste or cook to taste in a frying pan or grill.

Beef mince
Mix your own recipe of salt, pepper, herbs and spices with a little oil and mix into the mince. Leave for an hour. Spread the mince out on a shallow tray and place in the cold smoker for 1–2 hours. Remove and cook mince as required.

Hot smoked brisket
You can smoke brisket in a similar way to the pulled pork. Use a rub rather than brine or cure. Cover the meat in the rub and place in a marinating or plastic bag and refrigerate overnight. Do not rinse. There are several ways of smoking this:

- Place in a cold smoker for 6–8 hours, remove, wrap in a double layer of foil and cook for a further 10 hours at a low heat in the oven.
- Place in a cold smoker for 2–4 hours and then hot smoke at a low temperature for 10 hours.
- Place straight into a hot smoker and smoke for 12–14 hours at a very low heat.

Lamb

Lamb is best hot smoked and is one of my favourite dishes. I normally smoke a boned rolled shoulder. Brine the meat with your own recipe. For a normal sized rolled shoulder, brine it for 24 hours. Rinse and dry. Brush with oil and season if required (an Old Smokehouse speciality was a smoked shoulder rolled in fresh rosemary). Cold smoke it for about 6 hours and then hot smoke or gently cook in an oven. Wonderful served hot with an orange sauce! (Good served cold, too.) Alternatively you can brine, dry and oil the joint as above, and then place straight into a hot water smoker and smoke over a low heat for 6–8 hours. Make sure that it has reached the required temperature for the required time to ensure it is safe to eat. (See cooking guidelines on page 89.)

Mutton

Prepare in the same way as lamb but it is better cold smoked for longer 8–10 hours and then very gently roasted in an oven rather than hot smoked. It is also wonderful added to a hotpot.

Sausages

Most sausages need to be hot smoked. You can smoke almost any type of sausage (including vegetarian) – again it is purely personal preference. Ensure that if you are buying sausages you smoke the ones with the highest meat content available. You will find a significant difference in taste and smokiness between a low-meat content sausage and a high-meat content sausage. Sausages are easy to smoke and are a good food to start your smoking with. There is nothing quite like a sausage straight from the smoker – it is the first smoked food guests at Smoky Jo's sample and always whets the appetites for more..!

Don't limit your sausage experiments to the usual meats. Try game, chicken and even fish sausages. They all smoke well

Making your own sausages

If you are making your own recipe sausages, use two-thirds lean meat to one-third fat, ensure that you season it well, adding salt (to attract the smoke) and pepper as a base and then create your own recipe. You can add breadcrumbs to absorb and hold in the fat but, if cooked at a low temperature, the skins should not burst and all the flavour-laden fat should stay in. Leave to mature overnight before smoking.

Don't limit your experiments to just the usual meats – try game sausages, chicken or turkey sausages or even fish sausages, they will all smoke well! Remember, you do not brine sausages as the meat has already been processed and seasoned.

Hot smoked sausages (cold smoking first)
Place the sausages on a rack and cold smoke for 2–3 hours. This ensures that the smoke has penetrated the skin and flesh and will give a deep smoky flavour. Then either hot smoke or cook in your preferred way.

Hot smoked sausages (without cold smoking)
Placing the sausages straight into a hot smoker is a quick and delicious way to smoke sausages. You may not get the full depth of smoky flavour because food takes on smoke best at a low temperature and hot smokers get hot very quickly, minimising the opportunity for this to happen – but you will still get a great tasting product.

Simply place the sausages in a hot smoker and cook for between 15–90 minutes depending on the size of the smoker, the sausages and how full the smoker is. They will take about 15 minutes in a small stainless steel portable or stovetop smoker, and up to 1½ hours in a larger water smoker.

Fish

Salmon
Salmon is probably the most commonly smoked food after bacon. It is delicious either cold smoked and thinly sliced with a wedge of lemon, or hot smoked with a favourite flavour or sauce.

Cold smoked salmon
Easiest to smoke in fillets. Once again the weight loss is important, so weigh the fillets first – they need to have lost 20% their weight to ensure that they are safe to eat. It is advisable to keep the skin on but, if you have a fillet that has already

had the skin removed, reduce the brining time by 10%. If it is a particularly big fillet, where the flesh is more than 3 cm deep, carefully make a small cut in the skin. To salt the fish, sprinkle a layer of salt (and sugar if required) on the bottom of a tray or shallow dish. Place the fish skin side down on the salt and then sprinkle salt all over the fish, being careful to sprinkle much less salt on the thinner parts of the fish such as the belly and tail. I always liken the sprinkling to a light covering or dusting of snow with a little more on the fleshier parts of the fish.

Leave the fish to salt for the required time. For a 1–2 kg side the fish will need between 8–10 hours. However, if the fish has been frozen or is wild you need to reduce the brining time by about a third. A wild side the same size would therefore need brining for 5–6 hours.

The freezing process breaks down the cell walls of the flesh and therefore it absorbs the salt quicker. A wild fish will have had a very different life from farmed fish, with more muscle and less fat, and again takes on the salt more quickly.

After salting you will notice that the fish will be wet and sitting in the liquid that has come out through the process of osmosis – hence the need for a shallow (but edged) dish or tray. The fish will now feel firmer as it has lost the liquid and started to dry out.

Rinse the fish under cold running water, being sure to get all the salt off. Leave uncovered in a fridge or cool place to dry and mature overnight. Do not put a wet fish into the cold smoker. Smoke at a temperature below 25°C; if the temperature rises over 30°C your salmon will start to cook and may spoil.

Smoke the fish for at least 10 hours and anywhere up to 24 hours (or more!) depending on the size and what flavour you want to achieve.

Weigh the fish. If it has lost 20% of its weight it will be fit to eat. You will also know when the fish is sufficiently smoked and fit to eat when it has the rigidity of cardboard. It should lie completely flat across your hand – in fact you should almost be able to balance it on one finger. To be honest, I have used this method every time since the first smoking at the Old Smokehouse, when I did weigh the fish (see note on page 41 re: weight loss).

If the fish has had enough smoke according to your taste but has not lost the required weight, you will need to air dry in order to help it with the weight loss. See cold smoked venison for details of air drying on page 95.

My advice is to take out the pin-bones and belly-bones from the fillet after it has been smoked. It is much easier to see the bones and it will reduce any tearing of the flesh. Another tip is to put the salmon in the freezer for about 45 minutes before you slice it. This firms it up a little and makes it easier to cut those wafer thin slices.

There is now advice which came out from Seafish December 2011 that salmon that is not going to be cooked such as smoked salmon and sushi should be frozen either before or after smoking to kill parasites. Whilst this guidance was aimed at commercial production of smoked salmon I think it is something that we should be aware of. The note goes on to state that farmed fish are exempt if certified 'parasite free' and certainly most supermarkets publish that their salmon is 'parasite free'. I would advise unless you are able to guarantee the traceability of the salmon you are using, that salmon should be frozen either before you smoke it or after smoking and before consuming. The current safe legal advice is to freeze salmon at -20°C or lower for at least 24 hours.

Fish bones
If you have a whole fish and you fillet it yourself, don't forget to smoke the

bones! Brine them for one hour, rinse off, dry and place in the cold smoker with the fillet. Smoke for at least 4–6 hours. The easiest way to pull off the flesh is to scrape down the length of the bone with a dessert spoon. You will be amazed at how much flesh you will gather and this is excellent for smoked salmon pâté, adding to scrambled egg, quiches, etc.

Hot smoked salmon – (cold smoking it first)

Hot smoked salmon is becoming very popular, either as whole sides or more commonly served as fillet steaks. It is sold commercially under various names – smoked roasted salmon, braden roast (from the Irish for roast salmon) and salar smoked salmon (salar from the Latin name of the Atlantic salmon). Cover the fish with a dry salt in the same way as for cold smoking salmon, being careful to put much less salt on the thin parts of the fish than on the fleshier part of the fish. Leave it for 1 hour for a fillet, 30 minutes for a steak. Rinse off the salt under cold running water. If you are going to cold smoke the fish first before hot smoking it, allow it to dry or dry it with paper towels before putting it in the cold smoker.

The great thing about hot smoked salmon is that you can have fun developing your own recipes. My suggestion is to cover the top of the salmon with a flavour of your choice and then cold smoke it for 2–3 hours before hot smoking it or gently roasting it in an oven until cooked. We have had some wonderful flavours at Smoky Jo's – dill, Tandoori, lemon and pepper, lemongrass and coriander. Smoky Georgina's favourite is marmalade and cinnamon ... delîsh!

Hot smoked salmon – (without cold smoking it first)

This is a great way to smoke food. It may not have the full depth of cold-then-hot smoked salmon, but you still get a wonderfully moist, gently smoky piece of fish that takes only minutes to smoke!

I suggest that you use salmon steaks for this process. As you are going to put the salmon straight into a hot smoker without cold smoking it first, you will not have to worry about drying it before it goes in the smoker. Simply rinse off the salt, flavour the salmon if you wish and place straight into a hot smoker. In something like a stainless steel portable or stove top smoker the salmon with be smoked and cooked in about 8–10 minutes. Serve hot – perfect! – or cold – also perfect, and smokier if left to mature in the fridge for 24 hours.

Gravadlax

I am putting in a simple recipe for making Gravadlax. Many people think that this is smoked. It isn't, but it is cured and it makes a tasty and colourful addition to a platter of smoked fish.

Brush a fillet of salmon with oil, cover with salt, sugar and pepper mixture, then cover with a thick layer of dill.

Seal in cling film. If you have a vacuum packer then it is worth vacuum packing the fish as this will increase the weight on the fish. Place in the fridge or cold larder with weights on top – we use tins, bags of sugar or bricks (sealed in cling film)! Turn the fish every day. After 3 or 4 days, slice or freeze.

For 1–2 kg fillet - 3 tbsp salt, 4 tbsp sugar, and 2 tsp pepper.

For ease, slice from frozen.

Trout

Trout is generally hot smoked. In fact some books recommend that it is always hot smoked; this is because fresh water trout from non-running water may be more at risk of having clostridium botulinum (botulism) spores present, which only cooking at very high temperature destroys. Any risk is minimised as long as, once cold smoked, the food is eaten in the next day or so, or frozen immediately. As a fisher-woman I cannot resist cold-smoking a large trout if I am lucky enough to catch one. My rule is any fish less than 2 kg in weight always gets hot smoked. Any fish over that weight (very rare!) will be filleted and cold smoked in the same way as cold smoked salmon. I do tend to use a stronger brine solution for trout and I make sure they are well done if hot smoked and very dry if cold smoked.

Hot smoked trout (cold smoking first)

I do not fillet trout but keep the fish whole for hot smoking. Brine fish in your own recipe brine for 30–45 minutes. Rinse off under cold running water. If you are going to cold smoke the fish first before hot smoking it, allow to dry, or dry it with paper towels. Place in a cold smoker and smoke for 2–3 hours, then hot smoke or gently cook in an oven. Smoky Georgina tends to bake them at a low temperature for much longer than they need – more than an hour – to dry them out more ... her preference!

Hot smoked trout (without cold smoking first)

If large, may be done in steaks or fillets as hot smoked salmon.

For a whole trout, brine in your own recipe for 30–45 minutes. Rinse off and place in a hot smoker. Up to a 400 gm trout should be ready in about 15 minutes, depending on the size. The skin starts curling away from the flesh when ready – you can check by cutting into the flesh to ensure it is fully cooked. Serve hot or cold.

Sea trout

We had a lovely gentleman who came to the Old Smokehouse at the end of the fishing season with a crate of sea trout, and a week later he would come to collect about a hundred packs of the best smoked fish I have ever tasted. We obviously had to check the taste for quality control... In my opinion, smoked sea trout edges smoked salmon every time: it is stunningly good!

If cold smoking – smoke in exactly the same way as smoked salmon.
If hot smoking – smoke as for hot smoked trout, or in steaks as for hot smoked salmon.

Halibut

Fillet and salt for 4–6 hours. Cold smoke in the same way as cold smoking salmon

Hot smoked mackerel

Home smoked mackerel should be nothing like the mass-produced commercially available product and, if your mackerel is very fresh, will surpass your highest expectations! Gut them, but do not fillet. Brine in your own recipe (I suggest that you include some lemon juice for mackerel) for one hour. Rinse and, if you are going to cold smoke them before hot smoking, them let them drip-dry. Place in a cold smoker for 2–3 hours and then hot smoke or gently cook in an oven.

If the mackerel is going to be just hot smoked after brining, rinse it off and place in a hot smoker. Mackerel should be ready in about 12–15 minutes, depending on the size. Cut into the flesh to ensure it is fully cooked. Serve hot or cold.

Smokies – hot smoked haddock

Traditionally known as Arbroath Smokies, where they have been produced for many years using a very specific process – being almost steam smoked in a half barrel under damp hessian. I have seen them being prepared and sold as 'fast food' at Scottish shows! Any hot smoked haddock can be delicious, even if it is not quite the same as an Arbroath Smokie.

Hot smoke haddock in the same way as you would trout. Brine for 30–45 minutes. Rinse and, if you are going to cold smoke them before hot smoking them, let them drip-dry for a few hours. Place the fish in a cold smoker for 3–4 hours and then hot smoke or gently cook in an oven.

If the haddock is going to be just hot smoked after brining, rinse off and place in a hot smoker. Haddock should be ready in about 12–15 minutes, depending on the size. Cut into the flesh to ensure it is fully cooked. Serve hot or cold.

Herring – kippers
Smoked herring are best known as kippers, and are filleted differently to other fish. Cut the fish through the back of the head and down the back, ensuring the knife runs above the backbone to the tail. Open and gut the fish, being careful not to damage the belly wall. (Your fishmonger will do this for you.) Brine in your own recipe for 30–45 minutes. DO NOT RINSE. Allow to dry for at least an hour and then cold smoke for 5-6 hours. Place under a grill to cook.

Whitebait
These can be a bit fiddly to prepare but the finished product is well worth it. Make a small incision below the gill and squeeze out the gut. Rinse well. Brine in your own recipe for 5–10 minutes. Rinse and dry. Cold smoke for 3–4 hours and then either hot smoke or remove and grill or deep fry.

Tuna
Tuna is hot or cold smoked in much the same way as salmon.

Salt with a mixture of salt and sugar for 30–45 minutes and then cold smoke for 1 hour before hot smoking or cooking.

If cold smoking the whole fillet (called a ham or loin), salt for 10 hours. When using a large piece of the fillet or loin we tend to roll it (and re-roll it periodically) in a 2:1 mix of salt and sugar. You can add your own ingredients to the salt and sugar if required. Continue as with cold smoked salmon, cold smoking for 10–24 hours. Serve thinly sliced. All cold smoked meat and fish are easier to slice if slightly frozen.

Marlin and swordfish
Smoke as per tuna.

Shellfish

We love smoking shellfish. Scallops (both queen and king with the coral if liked), prawns, mussels, whelks, clams, cockles and langoustines are all delicious smoked.

It is recommended that shellfish are hot smoked or heat treated in some way to ensure they are safe to eat. The flesh is delicate so care must be taken not to dry it out.

Fresh raw shellfish is the ideal for smoking but we also cold smoke shellfish that has been cooked. The food seems to take on the smoke well and there is far less concern about food safety.

Never use shellfish with open shells as this means the fish is dead

For raw shellfish always brine in your own mild to medium recipe brine for about 2–5 minutes. Rinsing the fish is optional but dry and brush with oil before cold smoking for 2–3 hours and then hot smoke or cook in your preferred way. The raw translucent colour will turn to a more solid opaqueness when cooked. Avoid over-cooking as the flesh will become rubbery.

When smoking shellfish that has already been cooked, you do not need to brine. Rinse them (they usually have a salt glaze) and then carefully 'wring out' – there can be a high water content that you want to get rid of! Ensure that the fish is dry before placing it in a cold smoker. Cold smoke for 1–2 hours. Serve in your preferred way.

Squid and octopus

Ensure the flesh is fresh and tender. Use only the tentacles of the octopus, but the whole of the squid (particularly baby squid) can be used.

Brine in your own recipe for 5–15 minutes for squid and 15–30 minutes for octopus. Rinsing is optional. Dry and brush with oil to prevent the outer flesh drying out. Cold smoke for 3–5 hours depending on the size of the flesh. Hot smoke or cook in your preferred way.

Fish eggs – roe and milt

Both roe (female eggs) and milt (male eggs) can be smoked. This is a very delicate process as the thin egg sacs can break easily.

Weigh the roe. Brine in muslin in your own recipe brine (60–80%) for 1–5 minutes. Place in shallow dish and cold smoke for 6–8 hours. You are looking for a 30% loss in weight. If the roe has not lost its required weight after smoking, air-dry it until it has. See cold smoked venison for details about air drying on page 95.

Cheese

You can smoke almost any type of cheese. Nearly all cheese should be cold smoked at a temperature no higher than 25°C. If your cold smoker goes much over this temperature, your cheese will begin to melt.

The exception to this is halloumi, which can be both hot and cold smoked without ending up as a fondue on the bottom of the smoker! Halloumi can be a little salty but is a really good comfort food when hot smoked. It is also becoming very popular to have brie or camembert gently warmed in the box and this can be done in a hot smoker.

In order to reduce the staining from the shelves or racks in your cold smoker you can place muslin on the bottom of the cheese. This will allow the smoke through and protect the cheese.

Again, because the cheese has been processed and already has a level of salt in it, you do not brine cheese before smoking it. Place cheese on a rack in a cold smoker and smoke for between 6–24 hours, depending on the size, the type and your preferred taste. Softer cheeses do not need to be smoked for so long. Harder, more mature cheeses generally take longer to smoke.

As a very rough guide I smoke a wedge of brie for about 6 hours; a 500 gm piece of Stilton for about 8 hours, and a 500 gm slab of mature cheddar for about 12 hours.

You will not get the best taste out of cheese when it is straight out of the smoker. It is much better to take the cheese out and let it stand for a couple of hours. You will also see that the smoky flavour will continue to mature in the cheese for a while after smoking, so a cheese eaten 24 hours after smoking may well be smokier then when the cheese is first taken out of the smoker.

Remember, smoked food is all about taste – your taste. So experiment with your favourite cheeses, smoke them all for about 6 hours, leave them for 24 hours and then taste them. If you require more of a smoky flavour, put them back in and smoke for longer.

We smoke all types of cheeses, from mature cheddar and blue Stilton to Jarlsberg, ewes' and goats' to softer waxed cheeses (wax removed). Try them all – they are a great addition to a cheese board or for use in cooking to impart a lovely smoky flavour. Smoked cheese can, of course, be used as an alternative to any cheese in recipes for sauces, soufflés, quiches, dips and so much more.

Vegetables

Some vegetables smoke better than others and this is largely due to their liquid content. The higher the water content, the greater the risk of having a mouthful of smoky water – not good! For vegetables that are mostly water (such as aubergine or marrow) we do dry salt the cut flesh for a short time (30 minutes) before smoking. Apart from this, as a rule we do not brine vegetables, though we may just to add a flavour as a marinade – such as tossing mushrooms in a little salt, olive oil, black pepper and garlic before hot smoking them – rather than to get the salt to penetrate the flesh for smoking purposes.

There are no hard and fast rules for smoking vegetables. Not all vegetables smoke well – although that may be my palate! I prefer to cold smoke vegetables and then cook them (or not) normally as part of a dish or menu. For example, if you hot smoke peppers they are already cooked and you need to eat them on their own or mixed in a cold dish. However, if you cold smoke them you can put them in a salad, throw them in with other vegetables to roast, stuff and bake them etc – so I think that cold smoking gives you more options. That is not to say hot smoked vegetables are not amazing in their own right. Smoky Georgina, on the other hand loves hot smoked peppers!

Most vegetables just need to be properly washed, dried and put in a cold smoker for at least 2–3 hours depending on the taste required. You can then either hot smoke them or cook them in your preferred way.

I tend to leave the skin on vegetables, as the outer layer (the pellicle) of anything smoked is always a little tough and rather too smoky, so peeling them after smoking works well.

I prefer to cold smoke and then cook, but some people cook and then cold smoke. Smoking vegetables really is all about personal taste – there is little preserving value in smoking vegetables and I suggest you just have some fun experimenting. No right or wrong answers – just what works for you!

To help, here are some of the vegetables we regularly smoke.

Mushrooms

Mushrooms can be hot or cold smoked. My preference is to chop, season and put them straight into a stovetop smoker for about 8–10 minutes. One important point if smoking whole mushrooms is always smoke them stalk-side down. Otherwise, as the smoke dries the mushroom, the liquid that comes out collects in the cup of the mushroom and you can get smoky water. I tend to find the skin a little bitter so my advice is to peel them after smoking. Smoky Georgina, on the other hand, thinks that is a waste!

Different types and sizes of mushrooms smoke in different ways, so experiment

Also, if you peel (or not) and slice them, you can put them in jars then cover in olive oil. These will keep for longer and can make good presents, if you really want to part with them! Smoked mushrooms also make the most delicious mushroom soup.

Peppers

Lovely hot or cold smoked. Simply put in a cold smoker for 3–4 hours and then either hot smoke or cook in the preferred way. Again, if you peel and slice them you can put them in jars (making sure they are covered in olive oil) for storage or gifts.

Garlic

Garlic can be hot or cold smoked. Cold smoked garlic keep longer, retain their firmness and can be used in lots of different ways – in salads, dressings, stir-fries, roasted with other vegetables or on their own in soups, casseroles, etc.

When hot smoked, garlic goes beautifully soft and you can squeeze the flesh out of the skins and spread on to bread with olive oil, add to a creamy mashed potato, blend into soups, etc. Many times we've seen people surprise themselves by eating whole cloves from hot smoked garlic which they were supposed to be taking home from Smoky Jo's!

If cold smoking, you need to smoke them for at least 36 hours. They should be golden in colour. If hot smoking, you can either cold smoke them first and then hot smoke or roast them or put them straight into a hot smoker. They are ready when golden brown and soft to touch.

Tomatoes

Tomatoes can also be hot or cold smoked. We tend to hot smoke them and then serve them on their own as a side dish, add them to another dish or use them to make smoky tomato ketchup.

Simply wash and place in a cold smoker for 2–4 hours. Then either hot smoke or cook in the preferred way (also see page 138).

Tomatoes also smoke very well if cut in half, seasoned and put straight into a hot smoker and smoked for 10–15 minutes.

Onions and shallots

Smoked onions and shallots are delicious either served up on their own or added to dishes to give a hint of smokiness.

Remove the outer layers of skin until you get almost to the flesh and place in the cold smoker for 6–10 hours, according to preferred taste. Remove the rest of the skin and use in salads, pickled, roasted on their own or added to stews, burgers, etc. Smoked onions make the most sensational French Onion Soup.

Like tomatoes, onions also smoke well if skinned, cut in half, seasoned and placed straight into a hot smoker for 10–15 minutes. Alternatively, you can peel them and place them whole in a hot smoker for 30–45 minutes and serve them as a side dish.

Root Vegetables

We can recommend smoking all of the root vegetables – such as potatoes, parsnips, swede, carrots, turnips and also the more unusual ones like celariac and kohlrabi. They can be cold or hot smoked. We generally cold smoke them by putting washed but unpeeled vegetables in a cold smoker and smoke them for 3-5 hours or according to taste. These can then be cooked – boiled, steamed or roasted as per your usual cooking method.

If you want to hot smoke them it is often best to first peel them and par-boil, then whilst they are still firm put them in a hot smoker and smoke over a low heat for 20-30 minutes.

You can however also hot smoke vegetables quickly – just by peeling them and putting them in any hot smoker and hot smoking them until cooked.

Serve your smoked veg in the usual way or for something different use them in mashes, soups, and casseroles. Making side dishes as Potato Gnocchi or Potato Rosti are amazing when made with smoked potatoes.

Chillies

Many people now grow their own chillis and these are lovely dried or smoked as a way of preserving them and to add flavour. We cold smoke chillies by simply placing them in a dish or tray in the cold smoker, smoke them for about 4-6 hours and then freeze them. They can then be used in all sorts of dishes. One suggestion is to make chilli and garlic butter or put them in a flat bread such as a focaccia or in soups, casseroles, sauces, pâtes on pizzas – the use of smoked chillies is endless!

Asparagus

Smoked asparagus is a revelation! We discovered this simply by putting some in a stove top smoker with salmon. Easily cold smoked by putting it on a plate in a cold smoker for 30 minutes and then cook; or put in a hot smoker for about 20 minutes (or stove top smoker for about 10 minutes) until it is tender – (be careful not to overcook) and serve with butter or hollandaise sauce.

Marrow

You need to be careful when smoking marrows as they have a high water content so if you over smoke them they just taste of smoky water! So despite my earlier claim that we don't brine vegetables – with something like a marrow, cucumber or even courgette I will often split them and just rub a little salt into the flesh and leave it for about 30 minutes before brushing off the salt and cold smoking them.

Cold smoke the marrow for between 1-1½ hours or to taste and then remove the core, stuff with savoury mince and bake in an oven; or slice and steam, drizzle with butter; sprinkle with black pepper and serve!

Lots of vegetables smoke well. We generally cold smoke them and use them in cooking as normal – try them all.

Fruit

I can feel people starting to doubt anything written in this book when they see we are talking about smoking fruit! However, anything sweet, fruity and tangy goes really well with smoked food so I thought it stands to reason that smoked fruit should be good. I was not wrong – some smoked fruit can be amazing.

View smoking fruit as an experiment. We are still making it up! We leave the peel on and, for thick peel like bananas and oranges, we either slit the peel open or make cuts through it to let the smoke in. We do not brine fruit (though it will be worth sugaring some...) before we smoke it. So far I have cold smoked fruits prior to cooking them. Like the vegetables, anything goes and it is whatever you like that is right.

To help, here are some of the fruit we smoke.

Apples
Apples were a great discovery. Leave peel on and simply wash well, dry and cold smoke for 4–6 hours. These can then be peeled and eaten or cooked in your preferred way. Added to a crumble or apple tart, cored, stuffed and baked ... smoked fruit gives a surprising (and pleasing!) dimension. Smoky Georgina has promised a smoky tarte tatin with the next smoked apples...

Oranges
Wash thoroughly, dry and pierce the skin a few times. Place in a cold smoker for

6–8 hours. These make an interesting addition to fruit salad, sauces, gravy and home made marmalade.

In fact Smoky Jo's can claim a world 'first'. We won two Bronze Awards for our Smoked Orange Marmalade and our Whisky Smoked Orange Marmalade in the World Marmalade Festival. To my knowledge no one else had ever made a marmalade with smoked oranges (perhaps no one was crazy enough to think of it!) but try it. It is delicious. I now see that a number of chefs have cottoned on to this delight and smoked marmalade is being served in some top hotels!

Bananas
Smoked, brandied and baked bananas are a revelation! Split the skin down the length of the banana and prise the skin away from the flesh to allow the smoke to get inside the skin. Cold smoke for 4–6 hours. Eat, or use in any banana recipe from puddings to curries.

Damsons
Wash and dry the fruit and then place in a cold smoker for 4–6 hours. Stone and use in pickles, sauces or ketchup. One of my specialities is a smoked damson and smoked orange sauce which is amazing (even if I say so myself) served with slices of duck, goose, cold meat or cheese ... yes, I like it that much!

Cranberries
Wash and dry the fruit and then place in a cold smoker for 2–4 hours. Use in sauces, purées or as a garnish for game.

Lemons
Whilst smoked oranges may sound a bit weird smoked lemons certainly are not – they are absolutely delicious. Occasionally they turn up on the shelves of some of the top delicatessens but they are so easy to smoke that you may as well create your own.

You can cold smoke lemons simply by cutting them in half and popping them on a cold smoker for 1-2 hours. Our preferred way is to slightly hot smoke them over a very low heat for about 15-20 minutes so that they get slightly soft and maybe a little coloured by the heat and smoke.

Smoked oranges and lemons make delicious Candied Peel to add to scones, fruit cakes and other desserts

Fill the cavity of salmon or trout with slices of smoked lemon and discs of butter and grill or poach. Serve slices of smoked lemon with grilled Sea Bass, Plaice or Skate or to impart a fresh smoky and zesty taste. Drizzle smoked lemon juice over prawns or langoustine and then BBQ or grill. Oh and while you are about it – lemon curd and lemon marmalade or 3 fruit marmalade are all pretty special if made with half smoked and half un-smoked lemons!

Apricots

There are few fruits that smoke better than apricots. Cut in half and remove the stone and then either cold smoke them in a smoker for 1 hour or hot smoke for about 20 minutes in a hot smoker at a low temperature. If you want to smoke them in a stove top smoker you will only need to smoke them for about 5 minutes.

Keep in an airtight container and serve cooked with any pork dish, roasted chicken or Serrano Ham or Proscuitto or with confit of duck.

Grapes

Grapes take the smoke easily and we cold smoke them for about 30 minutes on a plate in a cold smoker and they are good sliced and added to something like a warm chicken and bacon salad or as an addition to a cheese board!

Dried Fruit – Sultanas, Raisins, Currants, Prunes etc.

These are lovely cold smoked and then added to dishes. Again like grapes they take on the smoke well so err on less time in the smoker rather than more.

Just cover a shallow dish with the fruit and place in a cold smoker for 1 hour or to taste.

Lightly smoked prunes go particularly well when added to a pork casserole or with braised pork fillet.

Smoked dried fruit is delicious added to baked apples, baked bananas, bread and butter pudding, apple strudel and so much more.

Use them in a 50/50 quantity with non smoked dried fruit when making fruit scones, fruit cakes, Christmas cakes or Christmas puddings and they are particularly delicious if you make your own mincemeat.

You will find other smoked fruit under the Smoking Gun section in Chapter 11.

Olives

Olives can be heavenly when smoked. Try your favourite type and flavour – there are so many! I like some much better than others but that is purely down to personal taste. Try any olives – whole, stoned or stuffed – until you find your favourites. We do not brine olives; in fact, try and smoke olives that have been kept in oil rather than brine as they can attract too  much smoke. (All olives have some salt content as they are generally all kept in brine after picking.) If you are buying them loose, always ask to taste one before you buy and avoid smoking any olives that are slightly bitter.

Prepare by rinsing and drying off on kitchen paper. Place in a shallow dish and cold smoke for 2–4 hours according to preferred taste. Use in cooking or enjoy with a glass of wine! (Lovely in a dry Martini!)

Nuts

We do not brine nuts but they can be improved with a light sprinkling of salt. You can smoke any shelled nuts; try them all until you find your favourites! We cold smoke them for a number of hours and serve as nibbles, or you can cold smoke then hot smoke or roast them for a few minutes and serve. Both are very tasty. In addition we sometimes flavour the nuts before smoking. Sweet or savoury flavours are both good on most types of nuts; we tend to flavour nuts like almonds with a sweet flavour (cinnamon and maple syrup) and nuts like cashews with a savoury (salt, garlic and chilli) flavour.

If you are going to flavour the nuts, it is a good idea to spray them with a little oil before sprinkling on the flavour to help it to stick on the nuts.

Spread nuts over the base of a shallow dish and cold smoke for 4–6 hours or according to preferred taste.

Eggs

There are a number of ways you can smoke eggs. We suggest you try them all and stick with the one you like best. Here are a couple of ways we smoke eggs:

Using eggs at least three days old (new eggs are impossible to peel!), place in cold water and bring slowly to the boil. Boil for 10 minutes. Take the pan off the heat and top up with cold water. Tip all the water out and refill with cold water. Repeat several times as this will stop the egg yolk edge turning black.

Peel the eggs and brine in your own recipe for 10 minutes. Dry and place in a cold smoker for 6–8 hours. They will develop a light golden colour.

Our favourite method is to use the same process as above but, rather than brine the eggs when peeled, we sprinkle them lightly with salt and pepper and then cold smoke them for 6–8 hours.

Smoked eggs are delicious eaten on their own or they can be used in salads, kedgeree, in the centre of a meat pie or in egg mayonnaise.

There are of course many more things to smoke – some more unusual than others. Turn the page to find out about our experiments into smoking the unthinkable........!

Chapter Eleven

Go smoking crazy!

Now, with our second edition of *Smoking Food at Home* and continuing on from the end of the last chapter, I want to share with you some of our experiments and also open up a whole new world of smoking food.

Since this book was first published we at Smoky Jo's have been pushing back the boundaries of smoking. We now smoke just about anything! – cold smoking that is and thanks to the Pro Q Eco Smoker cold smoking has never been easier. *Simply light the Cold Smoke Generator and fill up the Eco Smoker and it will burn away happily for hours gently smoking your food.*

There are lots of great foods that are not commercially smoked so you cannot buy them in a shop but with relative ease you can now smoke them at home. Most of these foods need to be put in a shallow dish – thus giving it the greatest possible surface area through which to absorb the smoke. Many do not need brining so it could not be simpler – just put the shallow dish in a cold smoker and smoke to taste. Our suggestion when experimenting is always to smoke for about 2-4 hours, take it out and let it rest for an hour, taste it and if you want it smokier than just pop it back in to smoke for a little longer. Like all smoking - have fun and experiment until you have perfected the product to your taste. Oh - and remember to keep notes as you go along!

Flour

We have recently started smoking flour to bake with! This has proved to be a great success. You can smoke any type of flour then use it to replace some or all of the flour in any of your favourite breads or pastries. It creates a subtle smoky hint that is delicious in Mediterranean-style breads such as sun-dried tomato or olive bread  or focaccia; lovely in cheese scones and extraordinary when used to make spicy mince pies or hot cross buns. You can use it to make pastry for savoury pies and tarts; smoked flour can also be used for making pasta, any dumplings and especially yummy if making beef or lamb cobblers, indeed anything you use flour for – as long as you like it. You can of course use a mix of smoked and unsmoked if you prefer.

Spread a layer of the flour about 2-3cm thick over the base of a large shallow dish to ensure the maximum surface area. Place in the cold smoker for 4-6 hours depending on strength of smoky flavour required. Stir the flour occasionally with a fork to ensure all the flour is exposed to the smoke. It will turn a pale golden colour.

Quorn and Tofu

These foods are designed to carry flavour. We have successfully smoked blocks of tofu and Quorn products without brining and these can then be used to create other dishes.

Simply place tofu or Quorn products in a cold smoker and smoke for 4-8 hours depending on the strength of smoke flavour desired.

Smoked tofu is great used in stir-fries, salads, pasta dishes, curries, noodles, kebabs, pasties and more.

Quorn is equally as versatile. You can smoke all the Quorn products – Quorn sausages, Quorn meat free chicken, Quorn mince. One of our favourite Quorn recipes is to smoke Quorn mince and then make tacos – the result is sensational. You can keep your beef mince – I will go for smoked Quorn mince every time for making tacos!

Salt

Smoked salt is finally becoming very popular and is readily available in most shops – it is a must in any kitchen. Use it any time you would like to add a gentle hint of smoke to your cooking. We smoke all types of salt, both coarse and fine – the list is endless.

Spread salt about 1cm thick over the base of a large, shallow dish. Place at the bottom of a cold smoker and cold smoke for 6-8 hours or to taste (the thinner the

layer of salt the less smoking time will be needed). Stir occasionally to ensure all the salt is exposed to the smoke. It will be ready when the salt has a uniform golden colour.

You can use smoked salt in so many ways. To season when cooking; to make your own flavoured smoked salts – by adding herbs and spices; smoke pickling salt to add flavour for curing and preserving; smoke rock salt for rolling baked potatoes in or encrusting or embedding meat, seafood or poultry for roasting. Again, anything you use salt for you can use smoked salt for.

Sugar

You might now be thinking that Smoky Jo has gone a step too far – but you could not be more wrong. Smoked sugar is a delight to behold! We generally smoke demerara sugar – mainly because it has quite a strong taste and is of course lovely and crunchy. It also holds the smoke really well but you can smoke any type of unrefined or refined sugar, white or brown.

Smoke it in exactly the same way as salt – 6-8 hours in a shallow dish and stir it once or twice during smoking to ensure that even take up of smoke.

We use smoked sugar in a number of ways – great added to a crumble (half and half with un-smoked sugar); we sprinkle it on baked bananas with a touch of rum or mixed with sultanas and a drop of brandy to stuff baked apples.

If you are making meringues and your recipe uses granulated sugar then use smoked sugar (muscovado or demerara are good for this).

You can also use smoked sugar in all sorts of baking and cooking – pastries and scones, cakes and biscuits as well sweets – a little smoked sugar in fudge is amazing as well as in glazes, dressings and marinades.

Blend 175gm of smoked sugar until it has the consistency of caster sugar then place in a pan with 100ml of water, bring to the boil and then cook for 2 minutes. Use to glaze buns, fruit scones, teacakes or tea breads as soon as they come out of the oven

For those more adventurous and artistic in their cooking, smoked sugar is great when used in making spun sugar for fancy desserts.

With all theses things if it is the subtle hint of smoke that tantalises your taste buds then think about using 20% smoked food to 80% unsmoked. Increase the percentage according to taste. People may not identify the smoke flavour but they will notice something deliciously different.

Herbs and Spices

We are now seeing some products like smoked paprika and smoked salts coming into our shops but you do not have to limit yourselves to these. Smoking herbs and spices is easy. Simply lay the food out on a shallow dish and cold smoke to taste. We usually cold smoke herbs and spices for about 2-4 hours – but try smoking them for longer if you want a stronger taste. Store in airtight containers or jars and use in the usual way in cooking.

It is hard to advise which herbs and spices smoke best – as it is completely about taste and what you like. I like smoked sage and oregano and I am not keen on smoked basil whereas Smoky Georgina really likes smoked basil but doesn't like smoked parsley – and neither of us like smoked mint! So again it is really up to you to experiment and try cold smoking or gently hot smoking any or all of the herbs and spices in your spice rack.

You can of course smoke powders as well as leaves. We have recently smoked mustard powder – ordinary English mustard powder - to which you add a little water to the smoked mustard powder to make a mustard paste. Roast beef with smoked mustard is amazing.

When cooking a gammon – use your normal recipe and before roasting remove the skin, score the fat and rub in a mix of smoked english mustard and brown sugar. Roast in the normal way – so good!

Pulses and Beans
All raw pulses and beans smoke well and are probably best cold smoked after they are soaked. Smoke in a shallow tray in a cold smoker for at least 2-4 hours, and then cook in your usual way.

Smoked kidney beans add an amazing flavour to a hot chilli con carne recipe; smoked chick peas and lentils make the most delicious dahl and there is little to match smoked chickpeas when making hummus.

Seeds and Grains
Along with herbs and spices we also cold smoke seeds and grains. These smoke in exactly the same way – in a shallow dish in a cold smoker.

You can smoke any seeds from sunflower and pumpkin seeds to fennel and mustard seeds. I do find that the larger seeds can become a little soft during the smoking process; this can be put right by drying them out a little in the oven after smoking or, better still, gently roasting them – truly delicious.

Use them in cooking your usual recipes or in salads, serve as nibbles or just have them handy when you get the 'munchies'!

You can smoke grains in the same way and if you are into brewing this might be something to try. On a less ambitious note even smoking a few oats can be fun. Add half and half smoked to un-smoked oats for baking such things as flapjacks or even add a few smoked oats when making porridge – topped with a little cream and some golden syrup – mouthwatering!

Syrups
Talking of syrups, these can also be smoked in the same way – a shallow dish in a cold smoker and smoked for 2-6 hours according to taste. Golden syrup, maple, mango and ginger all take on smoke really well. It can be a sticky process but the end result is well worth the mess.

These syrups can be used drizzled on either savoury or sweet foods. Imagine your Sunday breakfast, stack of pancakes, layered with bacon and liberally drizzled with smoked maple syrup.

Butter
Butter has to be one of our all time favourite smoked foods. It is simple, versatile and utterly sensational. I have become totally addicted to smoked butter and use it almost every day. Every kitchen should have a slab of smoked butter in the fridge.

I buy good salted butter (remember salt attracts the smoke); simply unwrap it but leave it standing on the foil and place it in a cold smoker. When we began smoking butter I used to smoke it for about 4-5 hours over beech but as my use has increased I am beginning to like a much stronger flavour so I now smoke it for 8 hours. I would suggest that you go for a milder smoke to begin with and see how you get on.

It has so many uses – but here are just a few. Fish – flash fry scallops, prawns and samphire. Sea bass or skate is lovely brushed with smoked butter; pack a trout or salmon with slivers of smoked butter and lemon before poaching.

Meat – smoked butter is wonderful for frying calves liver or minute steak or for frying onions and garlic as a base for a meat dish or gravy.

Smoked butter is fabulous when used to make hollandaise or béchamel sauces or even in a béarnaise or similar chateaubriand sauce, or used in any chicken dish such as chicken chasseur or even when frying chicken.

My favourite is to dip petals of a globe artichoke into warmed smoked butter — delish!

Corn on the cob dripping with smoked butter is so simple, but heavenly. You can add a little smoked butter on your new potatoes or steamed vegetables, along with some freshly ground black pepper to really 'wow' the taste buds.

Use smoked butter for baking – it is a great addition to any savoury pie, quiche or pastry, sausage rolls, pasties, samosas or cheese scones. The list is endless.

Cream

Why would you smoke cream? Because you can! It works well when used in either savoury or sweet recipes. I put it in a shallow dish in a cold smoker and smoke for 2-4 hours stirring occasionally. Refrigerate after smoking and if serving as cream on its own with a dessert, serve at room temperature to allow the flavour to be appreciated.

There are lots of other uses for smoked cream; smoked ice cream is a favourite – especially ice cream made with home grown summer fruits but as we know anything sweet, fruity or tangy goes well with smoke. Have some fun with other ice creams such as ginger, toffee, fudge or cinnamon.

Smoked cream is delicious in savoury dishes such as beef or mushroom stroganoff by adding a swirl to garnish a bowl of soup. Savoury mousses or soufflés can be enhanced with a little smoked cream. You can also use smoked cream for any cream based pasta sauce (I tend to use half smoked and half non-smoked) or in any sauce to complement a good steak.

Oils

You can now buy oak smoked olive oil in some good food halls and delicatessens. Lovely oils such as garlic, lemon, chilli, thyme, rosemary, sage and so many more are now on the market, and some of these are delicious smoked. Certainly many of the herb oils are great smoked and of course garlic is lovely along with one of my favourites – smoked lemon oil.

These are so easy to smoke. Simply pour into a shallow tray, put it in the smoker for 6-10 hours or to taste and just stir them every couple of hours to ensure maximum take up of the smoke. Store in bottles or jars. Any smoked foods make fantastic presents but to give someone a present of food that they cannot buy is extra special and what could be better than a jar or bottle of an unusual smoked oil?

Smoked oils are very versatile. We use them to cook with, use them in dressings and marinades, use them as a dipping oil with balsamic for artisan breads or even use them to keep vegetables in such as garlic, peppers, herbs etc.

We smoked a tray of truffle oil recently and just happened to have a side of salmon smoking above the tray of oil. I normally maintain that you do not get cross contamination of smells or flavours from different foods in a smoking chamber but oils are the exception on this occasion the salmon had a definite subtle flavour of the truffle - it was wonderful and something that we will experiment with further in the future (see, you learn new things every day).

Vinegars
You can smoke vinegars in exactly the same way. Try any vinegar – from white wine vinegar to balsamic and don't forget all the lovely fruit vinegars such as strawberry, raspberry, damson, mango etc. Store them and use them in the same way as oils. All oils and vinegars will smoke well – do experiment and have fun and I think you will be surprised at the outcome.

Hummus
We have mentioned smoked hummus before when smoking pulses and beans but if that is too much trouble then an easy way is to buy a good quality hummus and simply smoke it. Spread the hummus in a shallow tray and cold smoke it to taste – normally 4-6 hours breaking up the surface by stirring occasionally.

Gnocchi

We have mentioned smoked gnocchi before under smoked root vegetables but if making your own gnocchi from scratch is too time-consuming then shop-bought gnocchi will smoke just as well. Remove all wrapping and place on a dish. Place in a cold smoker and smoke for about 3 hours prior to cooking and then serve as a side dish, as an alternative to pasta with a cream or tomato sauce, or with sage pesto.

Packets and Mixes

Sometimes packet mixes are a godsend and can save you having to have a whole heap of ingredients that are rarely used and which go out of date before they are half empty. Well, these mixes can be smoked too! I have smoked a nut roast mix, cold smoking it in a shallow dish for 2-3 hours and then making it up and roasting it in the oven – utterly delicious.

Coffee

Subtly smoked coffee is an acquired taste and many people love it. You can smoke coffee granules, powder or beans. We like a good strength filter coffee to smoke but others enjoy smoking the beans and then grinding them for freshness. This is very much for personal taste so you will have to experiment to find your preferred length of smoking. I suggest that you start with just 30 minutes and build it up from there for your own taste.

Coffee and walnut cake made with half and half smoked coffee is one for the connoisseur.

The Smoking Gun

Lastly I want to introduce you to the Smoking Gun – this is a great bit of kit that is fun to use and will wow all your friends and family. We use it for smoking a number of different foods and liquids and it smokes in a slightly different way. The Smoking Gun is obviously a cold smoker and all it does is generate cold smoke that can be used to infuse a smoky flavour into liquid or to create a smoky environment for putting food in. These guns are increasingly seen in cocktail bars.

I would strongly suggest that you never immerse the smoke tube into liquid – you get a much better result from putting the liquid in a jug or bowl and covering it with cling film. Then by making a small hole in the cling film (I do this with the end of an extinguished hot match) you can insert the smoke pipe into the jug and simply fill the space between the liquid and the cling film with smoke. When you have done this take out the pipe and cover the hole with more cling film to keep the smoke in. Gently rotate the jug so that the surface of the liquid is moved or stirred within the jug and it will slowly absorb the smoke. After a few minutes the smoke dissipates and the smoking process is over.

The other way that I use the Smoking Gun is to put food in a zip-lock bag and then zip the bag along leaving a small gap at the end; then insert the smoke pipe into the bag through the gap and fill the bag full of smoke. When it is full, take out the pipe and zip up the bag completely. Your food will be immersed in the smoke and will slowly take on a smoky flavour. I have found that the smoke settles on the outside of the food in this process but that is often enough for some type of foods and some palates. Again the smoke will slowly dissipate leaving your food with a subtle smoky flavour.

Liquids

Smoking liquids is very easy – you can either smoke them again in a shallow tray in a cold smoker or you can smoke them in a jug or bowl using a Smoking Gun. It really depends on what taste you are after. I find that smoking liquids in a cold smoker for a couple of hours produces a milder smoke flavour and the smokiness lasts longer. Alternatively, infusing a liquid with smoke using a Smoking Gun is very quick and gives an instant smoky flavour which may not last that long and can sometimes be quite harsh on the tongue.

So if you are making cocktails, Bloody Marys, smoking vodka, red wine, mulled wine or even smoking water, the easiest way is to just put the liquid into a tray and pop it into a cold smoker. As with all other food smoked this way I would stir it occasionally and depending on taste you may want to smoke it for between 2-6 hours.

Water

Smoked water is now sold commercially but is very expensive. Save some money and smoke your own. Simply use the Smoking Gun to smoke a jug of water or place the water in a shallow dish and cold smoke for 2-4 hours. Store in an airtight container.

Smoked water is great for using in the bottom of a steamer when cooking vegetables. It can also be used to boil vegetables or rice. Poaching an egg in a pan of smoked water gives a different take on smoked eggs and is delicious. It is also useful for making stock or even for dissolving gelatine for making savoury jellies.

Do experiment with smoking water until you find a taste that you love – some people like it really well smoked while other prefer a much milder smoke. Strongly smoked water can of course be diluted.

Vodka and other spirits

Again smoked vodka is available in the shops now but smoking your own gives you the opportunity to smoke it to your own taste. Also unlike my advice about always using the best cuts of beef etc., when smoking I have found that many of the cheap spirits and wines smoke just as well if not better than the branded ones. Use the Smoking Gun or smoke in a cold smoker and serve as a Martini, soak fruit in it for adding to cakes or cheesecakes, take it with your favourite mixer or even mix with fruit jelly to make smoked spirit jelly shots.

Avocados

Here we are getting on to the second use of the Smoking Gun – smoking foods in a self-seal bag filled with smoke. This is a really quick way to impart a bit of smoky flavour to thin slices of food.

Using a large self-seal bag I place slices of avocado in the bottom and with the Smoking Gun I fill the bag full of smoke. Leave for about 10 minutes and then take out the sliced avocado. I sometimes sprinkle a little lemon juice on the avocado before smoking to stop it going brown as more often than not the food does discolour with the smoke. However it really doesn't matter and smoked avocado is delicious when making guacamole or avocado mousse or even putting a few slices into a warm bacon and chicken salad.

Mangoes

I smoke mangoes in exactly the same way – sliced in wedges and placed in a self-seal bag. Introduce the smoke with the Smoking Gun and then leave for 5-10 minutes before taking it out of the bag. The trick is to get a mango that is still firm – not too ripe but it must be lovely and sweet. Honey mangoes are by far the best but can be hard to find. A good Thai or Indian grocer will often sell the best mangoes.

Smoked mango is great to use in desserts like mango sorbet or ice cream. It takes on a whole new flavour when dipped in a rich dark chocolate (a must at Christmas time!). We sometimes soak it in rum and serve it with warm Jamaican Ginger Cake and cream.

Smoked mango is also good in salads with, for instance, prawns or avocado or served with Serrano ham and Mozzarella as a starter platter. Using smoked mango to make a salsa is delicious when served with either seared tuna or swordfish.

Strawberries and Raspberries
As we have made marmalade from smoked oranges so you can make jam, purées and sauces from strawberries and raspberries and other soft fruit.

You can cold smoke the fruit in a tray in a cold smoker for one hour or you can get a really quick smoky flavour by putting it in a self-seal bag and infusing with smoke from the Smoking Gun for about 5-10 minutes. Try both methods and see which one you prefer.

Tomatoes
We have covered smoking tomatoes earlier but I just wanted to mention them here as I often use the Smoking Gun as a quick and easy way to cold smoke sliced tomatoes. As with the other foods slice them and put them in a self-seal bag and fill the bag with smoke using the Smoking Gun. Seal the bag and leave for about 20-30 minutes. These smoked sliced tomatoes are now best cooked on top of a macaroni or cauliflower cheese; in a vegetable lasagne; added to a stir-fry on a steak or on a pizza. You can add them to a salad but some people might find them a bit bitter if eaten raw – but have a go.

Chocolate
Chocolate smoked correctly is absolutely delicious – smoked incorrectly or with the wrong wood it can be dire!

Again using a self-seal bag and the Smoking Gun, chocolate chunks or chips can easily be cold smoked. Leave in the bag for about an hour – or until the smoke has completely dissipated and then melt it gently over a basin of hot water stirring all the time before use.

You can also hot smoke chocolate by grating or chopping into small pieces and placing in a dish. Add it to a hot smoker and stir every few minutes as it begins to melt. We sometimes smoke chocolate in the stovetop smoker but it really only needs about 4-5 minutes after the smoke appears otherwise it becomes quite bitter.

Smoked chocolate is delicious in rich chocolate desserts, or as a sauce or when making a hot chocolate drink. A wonderful sauce is to grate chocolate and mix it with cream – hot smoke it until the chocolate melts and then whisk in a couple of dessert spoons of red wine – serve as a hot chocolate sauce or allow to cool and then serve.

Marshmallows
Marshmallows are lovely lightly smoked. I often do this when doing a smoking demonstration if there are kids in the audience.

Again using a small self-sealing bag, pop the marshmallows in the bottom and fill the bag half full of smoke and then seal it. The smoke dissipates quite quickly after about 10 minutes leaving you with a subtly smoked marshmallow that can be eaten straight away or served with ice cream and a fruit sauce or popped on the top of a hot chocolate drink or toasted on a stick.

…...................................

So there you have it – some of our little less conventional smoking ideas – which I hope have helped you to start thinking about all the other things you could have a go at smoking. The list is endless but try anything. Get away from the conventional and start thinking about what other foods might be tasty smoked. We love experimenting and hope that you will too.

And so to - smoked lasagne
I just want to end with a thought – how do you get the smoky flavour into some of your more complex dishes?

Well, the last few chapters have taken you through the step-by-step smoking of a huge range of food but when making a dish it sometimes becomes confusing as to which component part to smoke to introduce the smoky flavour.

Let me give you an example. I had a conversation recently with someone who decided to smoke a lasagne! So he made a lasagne and put it in a smoker and smoked it. It was interesting he told me – rather too much on the smoky side.

Well this got me thinking – if I wanted my lasagne to taste smoky how would I do it – and depending how you make your lasagne this is where the fun starts…

You could smoke the raw mince and then fry it to make the lasagne OR you could
Smoke the cheese and sprinkle it on top of the lasagne before cooking OR
Smoke the flour and make the pasta with smoked flour OR
Smoke the ready made pasta sheets OR
Smoke the flour and make the sauce with it OR
Smoke the butter and fry the mince in it and make the sauce with it OR
Smoke tomatoes and make the tomato sauce OR
Smoke water and make the stock with it OR
Smoke the milk or cream you use to make the white sauce with…

and so it goes on. I use this as an example to show that there are many ways to smoke, and cold smoking food and then using it in conventional cooking is a really easy way to get that smoky flavour.

So have fun, go mad and have a go; smoke anything and everything – remember as long as your food is safe to eat it is only wrong if you don't like it!

Happy smoking!

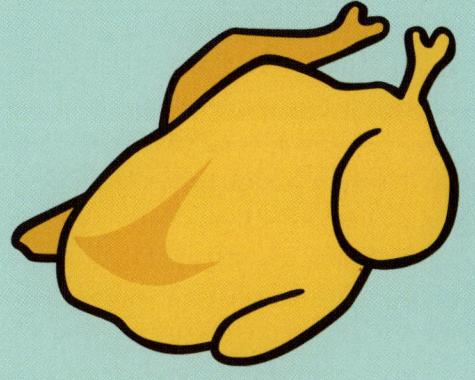

Chapter Twelve

Recipes and serving suggestions

We couldn't finish this book without sharing with you some of our favourite recipes and serving suggestions for smoked food.

The thing with smoked food is that it carries such complex flavours itself that, while there are some great recipes out there for smoked food, I think the majority of the time it is more about presenting and serving smoked food and selecting accompaniments rather than using smoked food recipes. When we first ran the Old Smokehouse, friends and family visiting for meals were invariably presented with what we called a 'grazing platter' of smoked goodies with perhaps a chutney or two and some crusty bread. We didn't have any complaints!

In this last chapter I want to help you make the most out of your smoked food. Here we share with you some of the different ways we at Smoky Jo's have used our own smoked food. They are more a collection of serving suggestions than anything else, but we have added in a few of our favourite recipes!

We also have a treat for you! In the winter months Smoky Jo's moves to the Wild Boar Inn near Windermere, a beautiful old inn with its own smokehouse. Our smoking courses there follow a slightly different format. At the Wild Boar, rather than tasting all the food at the end of the course, all the smoked food is taken to the kitchen. Our guests book in to the Wild Boar for the weekend and, after the course, we all gather together for dinner in the evening. Here, the food we have smoked is presented as an enormous 'banquet' of amazing dishes by head chef Marc Sanders and his team. So, in addition to our ideas, we have included a few of Marc's mouth-watering recipes.

How to get the best results from smoked food

Some foods are wonderful to eat straight from the hot smoker – sausages, for example. However, because smoke continues to permeate the food and flavours continue to develop long after it is removed from the smoker, it is often best to leave it for a few hours. Refrigerate within an hour and half of removing the food from the smoker. If not being re-heated, the best way to eat smoked food is at room temperature. If the food is taken straight from the fridge and is cold, you will lose a lot of the taste that comes from the wonderful smoky aromas and certainly some of the flavours brought out by the smoking process.

If you are serving previously smoked food hot, be careful to just heat the food and not to re-cook it, or you may dry the food. The best way to warm smoked food, particularly poultry and meat, is to wrap it in tin foil, add a tablespoonful of water (or wine, cider etc), seal it and then gently warm it for about 20 minutes or until piping hot. When warming fish use the same method but for 10 minutes, and you can also add a knob of butter, white wine or milk to the foil pouch.

All smoked food has its own distinctive taste and smell and can therefore be confidently served on its own with vegetables or salads, as a starter or main course or even a pudding.

Look to complement your smoked food with fruity and tangy flavours. The big flavours of American BBQ-style hot smoking, such as pulled pork, tend to be served smothered in smoky BBQ sauce. The best I have tasted was in a restaurant in Chester where the sauce had smoked bacon puréed in with the tomatoes and onions.

Be bold: serve your food with unusual fresh fruit to create something that will wow your taste buds and your family and friends. Our advice – as ever! – is to experiment and have fun.

It is always worth using the best ingredients if you can; use fresh herbs and spices. Mix your own preferred blend of peppercorns – not only does it increase the flavour, but pink, green peppercorns and pimento berries will add colour to a dish or sauce. High-quality oils and vinegars also make good essential basic ingredients for marinades, sauces and glazes.

So now you know that sweet and fruity flavours go well with smoked food, have a look at using some of these foods to enhance your dishes: papaya and cheese; avocado and chicken; mango and duck; fresh limes; spinach; plantains; yams; all varieties of green and mixed leaves; red onions; root ginger; jalapeno chillies; cinnamon; coriander; rosemary; teriyaki sauce; hoisin sauce; Worcester sauce; honey; maple syrup; oils; balsamic vinegar ... the world is your oyster sauce!

Of course there are lots more, and you will have your favourite flavours, but any of these ingredients can create tastes that will complement and enhance smoked food.

Serving Suggestions

Fish

- Serve cold smoked salmon, tuna or trout traditionally with lemon juice, freshly ground black pepper and brown bread and butter, with salad and hollandaise sauce or mayonnaise.
- Trout is lovely flaked on a bed of couscous – try lemon and coriander flavoured couscous.
- The gravadlax is beautiful served with a dill sauce or dill mustard, or cut into chunks in a salad, or added to a mild cheese sauce over vegetables such as broccoli or cauliflower.
- Hot smoked salmon fillet steaks are delicious hot or cold. Eat straight from the smoker, or they can be warmed in tin foil with a knob of butter and served with a salad. Whole sides make a wonderful centrepiece for a dinner party.
- One of my favourite starters is a slice of cold smoked salmon, a slice of cold smoked tuna and some prawns. The deeper pink of the tuna contrasts with the pink of the salmon and the gold of the prawns, making an aesthetically delightful, as well as a delicious, dish.
- Smoked salmon with scrambled egg – pieces tossed in for the last moments of scrambling or served on a hot plate under the eggs so the salmon warms up a little.
- Smoked salmon and Stilton quiche.
- Smoked salmon fillet steaks wrapped in puff pastry for a wonderful en croute.
- For a lighter dish, try wrapping them (warm) in a thin crêpe, sprinkle cheese on the top then put them under the grill to brown.
- Hot smoked salmon with a horseradish (and apple) crème fraiche.
- Smoked scallops with rocket, walnuts and a lemon juice and olive oil dressing.

Poultry

All smoked poultry can be eaten hot or cold in exactly the same way you would eat an unsmoked cooked bird, but here are a few suggestions to enhance the experience.

Chicken

It is wonderful hot or cold (ambient temperature). When warming it, try adding a teaspoonful of your favourite liquid in the tin foil to keep it moist. White wine mixed with the water, or even a drop of balsamic vinegar, will give you some interesting tastes.

A special tip: if you have smoked either a whole chicken or double breast on the bone then don't forget to boil the carcass for stock. Making soup from this stock gives you a wonderfully aromatic base, heavenly with winter vegetables.

- Hot with roast potatoes and vegetables.
- Add to a stir-fry.
- Try the chicken warmed and sliced in a salad, with mango and sesame seeds.
- Add to a casserole.
- On warmed foccacia with slices of avocado and a little garlic mayonnaise.
- Browned quickly on the BBQ.

Don't forget to make stock from the smoked chicken carcass

Duck

Duck breast is one of our favourites – but is also the one that is most prone to drying out when heated. You might like to try a drop of red wine in the tin foil with the water and then very gently warm it in the oven. Two minutes under a hot grill will help to crisp up the skin.

A single duck breast will normally be enough for four people for a starter if thinly sliced with garnish and served with an apricot and ginger chutney. The duck is wonderfully rich so serve it with delicate fresh or sweet flavours.

- Keep it simple – sliced thinly and served with crème fraiche and salad.
- Try serving it with a sweet red sauce, such as cranberry or redcurrant, or even with fresh grapefruit or satsumas.
- One of our favourites is to serve it with mango or papaya salad tossed with a spoonful of fresh lime juice.
- Remove the fat and reduce in a hot pan – fry slices of yam (sweet potato) in the fat and serve with the warmed breast on a bed of rocket and nasturtium leaves.
- My favourite – make a salad from mixed leaves, tomato, spring onions, cucumber, red peppers and toss in a raspberry vinaigrette. Place a smoked duck breast skin down in a hot dry pan, heat for about 6 minutes. Remove from pan and very quickly cut into rough cubes and throw into the salad – toss it well. The hot duck will slightly wilt the green leaves and blends

wonderfully with the fruity flavour from the raspberry dressing. Serve immediately. To yourself. No sharing!

Game

Venison

Try cold smoked venison cut into chunks and added to a casserole. It is cold smoked so you will find it will not toughen if cooked slowly in the oven.

- Serve hot or cold smoked venison as a cold dish; lay thin slices on a plate with a mixed leaf salad and rowan jelly or sliced apple.
- Cold smoked: spread thin slices sparingly with cream cheese and wrap around bread sticks – ideal for a snack or starter.

Pheasant

- Like smoked chicken and duck, smoked pheasant is lovely served cold with a salad.
- If serving it hot, a tablespoon of red wine added when warming definitely brings out the flavour of the bird.
- Rub the skin with half an orange and then place the other half of the orange in the pheasant while it is warming. Serve with an orange and sage stuffing.

Meat

Lamb

For me, there is not much to beat hot smoked lamb. Take locally produced rolled shoulder: we brine it for two days with herbs and spices, oil it, roll it in fresh rosemary and then very slowly smoke roast it.

- Served cold, sliced thinly, as a starter with garnish and an orange and rosemary jelly.
- Re-heat in the oven and serve as a traditional roast joint with mint jelly.
- Cut into strips and put in a stir-fry (avoid over-cooking!) with Chinese vegetables and flavoured with plum sauce.
- Our favourite is to serve it hot as a roast but with a tangy gravy made from cranberry sauce (the base), freshly squeezed orange, fresh rosemary and a hint of cinnamon – yummy!!

Ham

Smoked ham can be served hot or cold, and some say it should be served on its own to allow that taste of bygone days to filter through. However, if you do want to complement, fresh fruit will be great.

- Try it cold with an apricot and onion marmalade.
- Hot with a Madeira and apple sauce (also great with smoked black pudding).
- In your favourite flavoured stir-fry.
- In sandwiches with a mild mustard or mustard mayonnaise.

Beef

Both hot or cold smoked beef should be succulent and tasty. This makes it ideal for a starter or as part of a cold meat plate.

- Complemented (but not overpowered) by a horseradish and apple sauce.
- Spread thinly with red pepper relish, then roll around asparagus stalks as canapés or a starter.
- Another of our favourites – Carpaccio (very thin slices) of cold smoked beef, drizzled with truffle oil and then sprinkled with shavings of Parmesan. We didn't discover this gem of a recipe until about a month before we sold The Old Smokehouse ... another reason why we just had to start smoking at home!

Pork

Pork loin can be served hot or cold.

- Serve as steaks with mashed parsnip and a watercress salad.
- Serve on a bed of spinach that has been flash-fried in sesame or garlic oil.
- Delicious in sandwiches with sliced apple or mango.

Nuts

Smoked nuts – especially roasted – are a real comfort food! Try smoking all the varieties until you come up with your favourites. You can add flavours before you smoke them. You can use a sweet or savoury flavouring depending on your taste. We generally go for a sweet flavour on nuts like almonds, pecans and hazelnuts and a more savoury flavour on cashews and peanuts.

If using dry ingredients, spray the nuts with oil and then sprinkle your flavours on them before putting them in the cold smoker. This will help the herbs and spices stick to the nuts. If you are covering the nuts with a liquid like honey, you will not need to spray them first.

Here are some of the flavours we use:

- Salt, with or without freshly ground pepper
- Maple syrup or honey
- Maple syrup or honey and cinnamon
- Chilli powder
- Garlic granules
- Chilli, garlic and salt
- Tandoori
- Cajun
- Ginger

Experiment and come up with your own flavours; warmed through in the oven brings honey and cinnamon smoked almonds (my favourite) to near-perfection!

Sausages

Smoked sausages can be used in so many different ways: straight to the fork from the smoker or...

- In soups
- In a cassoulet
- In casseroles with garlic mash
- Cold sliced in a salad
- In stir-fries
- In sandwiches
- On pizzas
- Warmed in a salad
- In a pasta sauce – a tasty, meaty smoked sausage added to a tin of tomatoes needs nothing else!
- We slice them up and warm them in the oven as an accompaniment to roast chicken or turkey; they make a tasty change from traditional stuffing.

Cheese

We love smoked cheeses and we have smoked a huge range including: a strong mature Cheddar; a smooth creamy Lancashire; Shropshire blue and blue Stilton; Norwegian Jarlsberg; Brie and Camembert; Parmesan; goats' and ewes' cheeses;

cheeses with added fruit, vegetables or flavourings ... any cheese coming within range has found its way to the smoker!

None would be out of place on a cheeseboard, but we have certainly found some to be better than others. Even more than with unsmoked cheese, you will enhance the flavour of the smoked cheese by serving it with fruit – grapes in particular bring out the flavour – but apples, fresh apricots, pears or plums also work well. Our favourite is serving sweet pickled damsons with smoked hard cheese – it is sure to get great comments from your guests!

Don't forget to use smoked cheeses in your cooking. Use a little smoked cheese in a cheese sauce, or simply grate a little on top of the dish such as cauliflower or macaroni cheese. You will find the distinctive flavours add depth to most cheese dishes.

- Smoked Stilton and broccoli soup.
- Apricots mellow the distinctive flavour of the Stilton and, when mixed together, are a wonderful addition to quiches or savoury tarts (though, curiously, the flavoured Stilton with apricot cheese was not a big hit when we smoked it).
- Surprise yourself by adding a little grated smoked Parmesan to your dish – not a traditional way to treat this wonderful Italian cheese – but WOW! Once tasted ... hard to stop tasting...
- Try smoked Jarlsberg grated over Conference pears and toasted under the grill.
- Smoked Parmesan wafers – sprinkle a thin layer of grated cheese on buttered baking paper and bake for about 5 minutes.

Finally, here are just a few recipes that we thought we would include to show the variety of dishes you can prepare with smoked food.

Creamy Smoked Turkey Spaghetti

Serves 4

Ingredients:

1 tbsp butter
3 large leeks, sliced
1 tsp salt
150 ml chicken stock
150 ml thick cream
250 gms smoked turkey, roughly chopped
2 tbsp chopped parsley
$\frac{1}{2}$ tsp fresh-ground black pepper
350 gms spaghetti

- In a frying pan, melt the butter over moderate heat.
- Add the leeks and salt and cook, stirring occasionally, until the leeks are tender.
- Add the stock and simmer until the liquid reduces.
- Stir in the cream and bring to a simmer.
- Reduce the heat and simmer until slightly thickened, 2–3 minutes.
- Stir in the turkey, parsley, and pepper.
- In a large pot of boiling, salted water, cook the spaghetti until just done, spoon onto plates and serve creamed turkey on top.

Smoked Chicken Risotto
Serves 2

Ingredients:
- 200 gms risotto rice
- 600 ml chicken stock
- 2 tbsp olive oil
- 1 onion, chopped
- 100 ml white wine
- 1 large smoked skinned chicken breast, chopped
- 3 spring onions, chopped
- 2 tbsp mascarpone
- 2 tbsp grated Parmesan
- 3 tsp butter

- Add the rice to boiling water and cook for 5 minutes.
- Allow the rice to cool slightly, cover and set aside until ready to cook.
- Boil the stock in a pan. Reduce heat and simmer.
- Heat the oil in a pan, add the shallots and stir over medium heat for 3–4 minutes, until the shallots are beginning to soften.
- Add the part-cooked rice and stir well. Stir frequently.
- Add the white wine and bring to the boil.
- Cook, stirring occasionally until almost all of the wine has reduced.
- Add a third of the stock and cook, stirring occasionally until the rice has absorbed all of the liquid.
- Add another third of the stock and stir again until the liquid has nearly all been absorbed by the rice.
- When the stock has been absorbed, taste the rice to see if it is cooked but still firm. If not ready, add a little more stock and cook for a few more minutes.
- Remove the pan from the heat. Add the smoked chicken and spring onions and stir to mix well.
- Add the mascarpone, Parmesan and butter and stir well to combine and melt. Season to taste. Sprinkle with chopped coriander and serve hot.

Smoked Chicken Liver Paté

Brine chicken livers for 1 hour in your own recipe brine, rinse and dry. Cold smoke the chicken livers on a flat dish for 1–2 hours.

Ingredients:
> 500 gms of smoked chicken livers
> 1 onion
> 4 small mushrooms
> 1 clove garlic
> 1 tbsp brandy
> 2 tbsp soft butter
> 1 tsp mixed herbs plus salt and pepper to taste

- Toss the onion, garlic, herbs and butter into a pan over low heat and allow them to simmer until soft or slightly golden.
- Add mushrooms.
- Add chopped smoked chicken livers.
- Cook for 5–7 minutes.
- Once they are cooked, put mixture into a blender, add brandy and zap until it reaches the texture you prefer – it's smooth for me, every time!

Easy Cassoulet

Ingredients:

1 tbsp oil
1 onion, chopped
1 tsp fresh chopped garlic
1 tbsp mixed herbs
1 large tin mixed beans, drained and rinsed
1 large tin baked beans
225 gms smoked sausage, sliced
1 red pepper chopped
1 tbsp tomato purée
150 ml chicken stock

- Heat the oil in a large saucepan and fry the onion until browned.
- Add the garlic and herbs.
- Stir in the remaining ingredients.
- Bring to the boil.
- Cover and simmer for 20 minutes, stirring occasionally. (The smoked sausage won't spoil – the flavours from the sausage will permeate the whole dish, while the sausage becomes rehydrated.)

Smoked Haddock and Spinach Soup

Serves 4

Ingredients:

1 tbsp olive oil
2 large potatoes, sliced as thinly as possible
1 clove garlic, crushed
1 litre stock
1 large bag of spinach
300–350g cold (or hot) smoked haddock with skin removed
Grated nutmeg
Salt and freshly ground pepper

- Put the oil in a large saucepan over a low heat and add the potatoes and garlic. Cook for 10 minutes, making sure the potatoes and garlic don't brown.

- Add the stock, bring to the boil. Add nutmeg, salt and pepper to taste.
- Reduce the heat and simmer gently until the potatoes are cooked (5 minutes or so).
- Add the spinach and cook for another 1–2 minutes until the spinach has just wilted. Remove from the heat and give it a good stir.
- Add the soup to a blender in batches and pulse to liquidise.
- Return the soup to the saucepan and reheat slowly over a low heat. At this point, taste.
- Gently add cold smoked fillets of fish and leave them to poach without stirring for 3–4 minutes.
- Once the fish has cooked (just turned opaque throughout) gently break up the fillets into large chunks. (If hot smoked or previously cooked, add to soup in chunks and allow to warm through.)
- Add the lemon juice. Taste and adjust with more salt and pepper or a squeeze more lemon.
- Serve piping hot with a sprinkle of lemon zest.

Smoked Salmon Quiche

Ingredients:
>   200 gms smoked salmon, sliced into small pieces
>   3 eggs
>   180 ml single cream
>   120 ml milk
>   60 gms of cheddar cheese plus a little extra for sprinkling (you could use smoked cheddar to sprinkle)
>   1 tomato, finely sliced
>   1/2 tsp of sea salt
>   Freshly ground black pepper
>   1 tbsp finely chopped dill
>   2–3 sheets of store-bought puff pastry

- Pre-heat the oven to 180° C (350°).
- Defrost pastry if necessary and set aside. Lightly grease a 22cm flan dish.
- Make your filling by combining the eggs, cream, milk, cheese, salt, pepper and chopped dill together in a large jug. Whisk mixture thoroughly and set aside.
- Roll out pastry and line the dish and trim.
- Layer the salmon pieces in a layer on the pastry.

- Layer the sliced tomato over the salmon.
- Give the egg mixture another quick whisk before spooning over the tomato then sprinkle a little extra cheese over the top.
- Bake for 20–25 minutes or until firm and golden.
- Remove from oven and cool for 5 minutes in the tin then transfer to a wire rack to cool further.

Smoked Trout Kedgeree

Ingredients:

    300 gms long-grain white rice
    1 litre vegetable stock
    4 eggs
    1 tbsp extra virgin olive oil
    1 large onion, finely chopped
    1 fresh red chilli, seeded and sliced
    1 tbsp korma curry paste
    3 tbsp Greek-style yogurt
    280 gms smoked trout fillets, skinned and flaked into large pieces
    4 tsp chopped fresh coriander
    55 gms (2 oz) toasted flaked almonds
    Salt

- Put the rice in a pan, add the stock or water and bring to the boil.
- Stir, then cover and simmer very gently for 10–15 minutes or until the rice is tender and has absorbed all the liquid.
- While the rice is cooking, place the eggs in a small pan of water and bring to the boil.
- Remove from the heat and leave to stand for 2 minutes, then drain off the water.
- Cover with fresh cold water, and leave until cool enough to handle.
- Peel the eggs and cut each one in half.
- Heat the oil in a large frying pan, add the onion and chilli and cook, stirring frequently, for 10 minutes or until the onion is soft and has started to turn golden.
- Add the curry paste and cook, stirring, for 1 minute.
- Tip the rice into the frying pan.
- Add the yoghurt and toss together until well blended.
- Mix in the smoked trout, coriander and almonds.
- Replace on heat briefly and serve.

Smoked Scallops and Chorizo

- ❧ Slice chorizo and place in a hot dry pan. Fry gently, add a dash of oil and put cold smoked scallops in the pan. Flash fry. Season with salt, pepper and a dash of lemon juice.
- ❧ Serve on a bed of fresh spinach.

Smoky Cauliflower Cheese
Serves 4–6 as a side dish

Ingredients:

    1 medium cauliflower
    2 oz butter
    2 oz plain flour
    1 level tsp mustard powder
    Large pinch salt
    460 ml milk
    50 gms smoked cheddar (or other melting smoked) cheese grated, plus extra for sprinkling on top
    Freshly ground pepper

- Cut the florets off the stem. Peel the outer layer of the stem and finely slice. Steam the cauliflower over a pan of boiling water for 10 minutes. Remove the cauliflower from the heat and leave to cool.
- Place the butter and flour into a large saucepan. Over a low heat, stir the butter and flour until the butter has melted and the flour is incorporated. Add the salt and mustard powder and continue stirring for 2 minutes.
- Add the milk and stir vigorously until a smooth sauce is formed. Continue stirring until the sauce is thickened and glossy (about 5 minutes).
- Add the smoked grated cheese and stir until melted. Remove from the heat.
- Place the cauliflower in a baking dish large enough to hold all the florets in one layer.
- Pour the thickened cheese sauce over the cauliflower, ensuring all the florets are covered. Sprinkle with grated cheese and a good twist of black pepper.
- Bake in a hot oven until the sauce is bubbling and golden brown on the top, approximately 30 minutes.

Smoked Jarlsberg, Fruit and Fennel Salad
Serves 4 as a main course

Ingredients:

400 gms smoked Jarlsberg, cubed
1 apple, thinly sliced
2 fennel
$1/2$ red onion
2 tbsp olive oil
2 tsp chopped chives
$1/2$ chilli, seeds removed, finely chopped
Juice of 1 lime
Salt and pepper

Cut fennel in two and boil it in water for a couple of minutes, leave to cool. Thinly slice the fennel and mix with the red onion, apples and cheese. Make a dressing from the remaining ingredients, pour over salad, toss and serve.

Tea-Smoked Tomatoes

Ingredients:

8 large tomatoes, cut in half and seasoned with sea salt and pepper and a sprinkle of mixed herbs

Smoking mix:

Good quality tea leaves (jasmine is my favourite)
1 cup raw rice
1 tbsp brown sugar

- ❧ Put smoking mix in bottom of the smoker (stovetop, portable or a wok lined with foil).
- ❧ Place a rack in the smoker, place the seasoned tomatoes on it and place lid on.
- ❧ Place on heat for 10 minutes.

Smoky Tomato Ketchup

Ingredients:

> 2.5kg smoked tomatoes
> 4 tbsp Sugar
> 1 tbsp English mustard powder
> 1 tsp ground allspice
> 120ml cider vinegar
> 1 tsp salt
> 100g tomato purée
> 1/2 tsp black pepper
> 1/2 tsp ground cloves
> 1/2 tsp lemon juice

- Cold smoke tomatoes for 2 hours.
- Blanch and soak for 5 minutes in boiling water to soften.
- Strain through sieve to remove skin and pips.
- Add to all remaining ingredients and place in a pan.
- Bring to the boil and simmer for 2 hours.
- Remove from heat and allow to cool for 10 minutes.
- Put in warmed sterilised jars.
- Best kept in the fridge.

Smoked Stuffed Peppers with Goats Cheese

Ingredients:

> 4 large cold smoked red or orange peppers
> 4 large mushrooms chopped
> 50 gms couscous
> 100 ml hot vegetable stock
> 250 gms hard goats cheese, cut into cubes
> 2 tsp chopped fresh coriander
> 1/2 tsp Paprika
> 1/2 tsp mixed herbs
> Salt and pepper to season

- Preheat the oven to 200°C/Gas 6.

- Cover mushrooms in olive oil and sprinkle with salt, pepper, herbs and paprika.
- Cut the smoked peppers in half through the stalks and remove the seeds.
- Put the peppers on a baking tray.
- Drizzle a little of the mushroom oil over the peppers, then sprinkle with salt and pepper.
- Bake for 20–25 minutes, until the peppers are just tender.
- Tip the couscous into a bowl and pour in the hot stock.
- Leave for 5 minutes to soak, and then fluff up with a fork.
- Stir in the mushrooms, goats' cheese and coriander.
- Spoon into the pepper halves.
- Return to the oven for 10 minutes.

This recipe can also be made using halloumi cheese.

Smoked Egg Toadstools – a starter guaranteed to make your guests smile!

Serves 4 as a starter

Ingredients:

4 smoked eggs
2 tomatoes
Mayonnaise
Paprika
Parsley

- Hard boil, shell and smoke the eggs.
- Flatten by slicing off the tips.
- Spread mayonnaise in a circle on a serving dish, sprinkle with paprika and parsley.
- Stand the eggs upright in the middle of the mayonnaise.
- Halve tomatoes, sprinkle cut side with salt and pepper and pierce with cocktail stick.
- Use the other end of the stick to secure each tomato to an egg, and then dot the tops with more mayonnaise.

Ideas from the Wild Boar Inn, Grill and Smokehouse, courtesy of Head Chef Marc Sanders.

The Wild Boar is the wonderful old coaching inn at Crook, near Windermere, where we run our Smoky Jo's courses during the winter.

Smoked Stilton – served on Melba toast
Blend 200 gms of smoked Stilton in a food processor until it becomes a paste then add single cream to desired consistency. Take care not to over-mix or it will split.

Aioli – perfect with smoked trout
Mix mayonnaise with chopped (smoked) garlic, lemon juice and fresh chopped parsley

Tomato Chutney - to complement smoked sausages

Boil together:
>   1 kg ripe tomatoes, chopped
>   450 gms onions, chopped
>   2 garlic cloves, finely chopped
>   2 eating apples, peeled, cored and roughly chopped
>   2 tsp mustard
>   200 gms brown sugar
>   600 ml malt vinegar

Caper and Red Onion Salsa – gives cold smoked salmon a real kick!
Chop equal amounts of capers and red onions; add a splash of red wine vinegar, olive oil and coarse-grain mustard.

Black Pudding Mash
Chop and crumble smoked black pudding into mashed potatoes to lift both humble dishes to elevate them to something really special! Serve with any meaty dish.

Smoked Marrowbone

The marrowbone is split lengthways down the centre and lightly sprinkled with salt prior to cold smoking for a couple of hours.

Fry some chopped shallots in butter until soft, add chopped garlic, take off the heat and add breadcrumbs and chopped fresh herbs, salt and pepper.

Press the mixture onto the marrowbone and bake in the oven. This was the first time I had tried marrowbone and it was melt-in-mouth-magical!

Smoked Chicken on Waldorf Salad

Waldorf salad: finely dice equal amounts of celery and Granny Smith apple, mix with mayonnaise and crushed walnuts. Slice or cube smoked chicken and add to the salad.

Smoked Trout Mousse – on Melba toast or crostini

Put a skinless and boneless hot smoked trout fillet in a food processor and mix until it becomes like a paste, then add lemon juice, Worcester sauce, salt and pepper to taste, and finally single cream to desired consistency. Take care not to over-mix or it will split.

165

Smoked Damson Sauce – perfect with ham, including smoked ham, of course!
Boil together onion, smoked damsons, chilli, chopped tomatoes, lemon juice, cola, fennel seeds, cumin and garlic, then blend in a food processor.

Smoky Tapenade – sets off any fish dish!
Blend together smoked olives, smoked garlic and smoked almonds in a food processor.

Smoked Scallops and Black Pudding
Flash fry cold smoked scallops with smoked black pudding before adding a drizzle of olive oil and a splash of sherry vinegar to the pan and serving.

Baked Smoked Scallops and Smoked Black Pudding
Cold smoked queen scallops fried in butter with the smoked black pudding and strips of smoked pancetta. Coat with hollandaise sauce and bake in the oven. This is my favourite!

Smoked Mussels
Serve on salad leaves with vinaigrette – in a cleaned sardine or anchovy tin, Wild Boar style!

A note about food safety from Smoky Georgina

When I first started learning about food smoking, I was alarmed at all the food safety issues but there is a big difference between commercially smoking food for selling with a long shelf-life to the public and smoking food at home for ourselves. As with so many things, common sense is the key; if applied, your food will be safe and delicious!

Salt removes water from food, which helps preserve it. Smoke contains disinfectant, antioxidant and many antimicrobial compounds, which help preserve food. With the arrival of refrigeration, temperature control replaced salting and drying as means of food preservation. When smoking food for flavour it is sensible to pay attention to temperatures when salting, brining drying and smoking.

Fresh meat and fish should be stored under 5°C. Once above this, bacteria multiply more quickly and food starts to go off. When the food begins to be processed – i.e. salted or brined, bacteria activity is slowed or halted. As this process begins, it is usually fine to do this at ambient temperature. However the factors to consider are:

1. How warm is it? – If very warm, chill your brining food.
2. How big is the piece of food? – If very big, the middle will warm up before the salt reaches it, so chill and/or use a stronger brine for a shorter time.
3. How strong is the brine? – A stronger brine starts the curing more quickly.
4. Am I hot smoking or cooking the food after salting? – This will kill any bacteria that is still active.
5. How long will it be at this temperature? – A short brine is not going to allow food straight from the fridge to warm up enough to cause a problem.

So, if I were brining a 2 kg piece of food for hot smoking in the height of summer, I would brine it in the fridge, or put (and replace as necessary) ice packs in the brine.

If I were dry salting a side of salmon for cold-smoking for 8 hours I would be less concerned about the temperature. I would want it in a relatively cool place, but the dry salt is in direct contact with the surface of the food which would begin to dry immediately.

If I were brining chicken fillets in a 40% brine for 3 hours I would not worry about refrigeration.

Brining a large piece of beef on a warm day for cold smoking, I would use a stronger brine (60 or 80%) and keep it cool.

Many people produce wonderful cured meats in much warmer places than the UK without refrigeration. Our confidence has come with experience but if you have any concerns, use a fridge or ice packs, stronger brines and the addition of a small amount of saltpetre.

Once smoking, if you are going to hot smoke or cook your food immediately after the cold smoking process, temperature control is not an issue providing the food has been salted (or brined) and the smoke is moving around the food with a reasonable air flow. If the food is just being cold smoked however, you do want to keep the temperature below 25°C (30°C as an absolute maximum). You can put ice packs in the smoker, if necessary. Even running The Old Smokehouse in Cumbria there were some hot times when we could only smoke our salmon overnight!

Once hot smoked or cooked, food should be allowed to cool and refrigerated within 1½ hours.

Treat your home-smoked meat and fish as though it were cooked food – wrap it up and refrigerate or freeze.

We have had hundreds of people on Smoky Jo's courses over the last few years – some professional chefs, some enthusiastic amateurs, some rustic smallholders. Some prefer meticulous instructions for every ingredient, temperature and timing; others have hung vaguely home-cured legs of pork in trees for months! We have learned from them all and strive to maintain a safe, common-sense middle line.

A reminder of cooking times and temperatures:
These are times and core temperatures required to cook meat to kill E coli 0157, Salmonella and Listeria:

- 60°C for 45 minutes, or
- 65°C for 10 minutes, or
- 70°C for 2 minutes, or
- 75°C for 30 seconds, or
- 80°C for 6 seconds.

List of suppliers of home food smokers, wood and accessories.

Smoky Jo's

A range of smokers, woods and smoking accessories is available from Smoky Jo's.
Castle Court, Shap, Penrith. Cumbria. CA10 3LG
Tel: +44 (0)1931 716638 info@smokyjos.co.uk www.smokyjos.co.uk

Landmann

Supplier of the Tennessee Barrel Smokers, BBQs and a range of accessories.
Landmann UK: Landmann Ltd, Unit 6 Blackstone Road, Stukeley Meadows,
Huntingdon. PE29 6EF
Tel: +44 (0)1480 421720 sales@landmann.co.uk www.landmann.co.uk

Mac's BBQ Ltd

Supplier of the Cold Smoke Generator, ProQ Water Smokers and a range of
other smokers, BBQs and accessories.
Mac's BBQ ltd, Unit 3A, Rosevear Road Industrial Estate, Bugle, Cornwall
PL26 8PJ
Tel: 0845 519 4783 ian@macsbbq.co.uk www.macsbbq.co.uk

Cookequip Ltd

Supplier of the Cameron Stovetop Smoker and a range of smoking, BBQ and
cooking accessories.
Cookequip Unit 4, Sumner Place, Addlestone, Surrey KT15 1QD
Tel: +44 (0)1932 841171 sales@cookequip.co.uk www.cookequip.co.uk

Bradley Ltd

Supplier of the Bradley Electric Smoker, wood bisquettes and Bradley
accessories.
Tel: 01803 712712 info@bradleysmoker.co.uk www.bradleysmoker.co.uk

Index

Index